WAR
AT
WORK

SUN TZU'S *ART OF WAR*
WAR AT WORK

Applying Sun Tzu's *Art of War* in today's business world

KHOO KHENG-HOR

Pelanduk
Publications

Published by
Pelanduk Publications (M) Sdn. Bhd.,
24 Jalan 20/16A, 46300 Petaling Jaya,
Selangor Darul Ehsan, Malaysia.

All correspondence to:
Pelanduk Publications (M) Sdn. Bhd.,
P.O. Box 8265, 46785 Kelana Jaya,
Selangor Darul Ehsan, Malaysia.

All rights reserved.
Copyright © 1990 Khoo Kheng-Hor.
Cover design © 1994 Pelanduk Publications (M) Sdn. Bhd..
No part of this book may be reproduced in any form or by any means without prior permission from the Publisher.

ISBN 967-978-340-5

1st printing 1990
2nd printing 1992 (revised)
3rd printing 1993
4th printing 1994
5th printing 1995
6th printing 1996

Printed by
Eagle Trading Sdn. Bhd.

*Dedicated to my wife, Judy,
who besides exercising much tolerance, has also
been largely instrumental in teaching me the
actual meaning of the word.*

CONTENTS

Acknowledgements *ix*
Preface to the First Edition *xi*
Preface to the Second Edition *xii*
The Author *xiii*
Introduction *xv*

PART I
Applying The *Art Of War* 1

PART II
The Full Text Of The *Art Of War* 65
    Chapter 1   *Planning* 67
    Chapter 2   *Waging War* 70
    Chapter 3   *Offensive Strategy* 73
    Chapter 4   *Tactics* 76
    Chapter 5   *Energy* 79
    Chapter 6   *Weak And Strong Points* 81
    Chapter 7   *Manouevres* 85
    Chapter 8   *Tactical Variations* 89
    Chapter 9   *On The March* 91
    Chapter 10   *Terrain* 96
    Chapter 11   *The Nine Varieties Of Ground* 100
    Chapter 12   *Attack By Fire* 107
    Chapter 13   *'A Crack Between Two Doors' (Espionage)* 110

PART III
Application By Famous Characters 115

ACKNOWLEDGEMENTS

This book is only possible because I am fortunate to have had the assistance or encouragement in one form or another from several persons. Although it would be virtually impossible to list all of them here, some of them must be singled out and credited because of the magnitude of their contributions.

My primary thanks go to my wife, Judy, for helping with the tedious translation of those works in Chinese such as *Sun Tzu Shih San P'ien Chiao Chien Chi Yao* and *Sun Tzu Ping Fa*. I am also grateful to my nephew-in-law, Professor Tsai Ker-Jung of Taiwan's Political University, for sourcing and sending me materials that proved immensely useful.

I thank Mr Ian F. Bird, the former Director of MBA Programmes at the University of Stirling, Scotland, who not only encouraged me to write this book but also boosted my confidence in this project by his offer of a place to do a Masters in Business Administration at the university.

My thanks also go to Ms Zarin Steven-Johan, the former editor of *Corporate World* magazine, who not only planned to do an article on my passion with Sun Tzu's philosophy in the September 1990 issue, but also gave me her encouragement to make this project a reality. Mr A. Sri K. Nayagam, the assistant editor of *The Malay Mail* has also contributed much in reviewing and editing the manuscripts.

While I appreciate my former managers for their positive reception to applying Sun Tzu's philosophy in the workplace, my special thanks go to my former boss, Mrs S. K. Chan, without whose confidence and support, none of this would have come about in the first place.

PREFACE TO THE FIRST EDITION

Most working persons will tell you that the workplace is often like a battlefield. There is always this urgent need to keep ourselves updated on what our business competitors are up to, sending our people to clinch the deals before theirs do, throwing 'red herrings' to our business rivals, bringing on or defending against legal suits, etc. And of course, the inevitable daily office politics which most of us are aware of, though some may not care to admit its existence.

As I explained to my wife once when she complained that I have not been attentive to the way she looks or dresses: such details would usually not have escaped my attention at the workplace as my senses are finely honed to watch out for any anomaly, but at home, well, I feel safe ... I am no more 'at war' and therefore, I can afford to let my guard down.

As a student of the works of the 500BC military strategist, Sun Tzu, as contained in his book, *Art of War*, I have often marvelled at how applicable his lessons are to contemporary business as they are to war. But given his era – 2,500 years ago – it is often not easy to relate his philosophy to modern-day activities. However, much inspired by Sun Tzu, I have been sharing my interpretation of his works with my team of managers.

While I do not claim to be an expert, I have been encouraged by the response from those who have shared my interpretations and this has led me to compile my notes into this book and in this way share some of my thoughts with the others who inevitably find themselves having to 'fight it out' daily in the corporate and business 'battlefields' of today with the aim of improving

Preface To The First Edition

their productivity, profitability, working environment and interpersonal relationships. I have thus aptly called this book, *War At Work*, which can mean the warfare one has to face daily at the workplace, or the workability of Sun Tzu's principles in the *Art of War*.

Khoo Kheng-Hor
August 1990

Preface To The Second Edition

In addition to my original work, I have included two more sections; Part II and Part III, into this new edition. It is my sincere hope that after reading through the original text of Sun Tzu's *Art Of War* and the stories of how his treatist was applied, the reader would be able to better understand how the spirit of Sun Tzu's principles is still applicable even today.

Khoo Kheng-Hor
November 1991

THE AUTHOR

As a business executive, consultant, author and speaker, Khoo Kheng-Hor has been described as a contemporary interpreter of Sun Tzu's treatise, *Art of War*. He has been interviewed on television and newspapers for his creative interpretations of Sun Tzu's war principles for use, not only in strategic management but also in specific areas of management such as marketing, customer service and human resource management, and now corporate politics.

Besides being the Managing Director of Stirling Training & Management Consultants Pte. Ltd., his own firm which assists clients in planning and implementing strategies and motivating their executives through his specially-developed "Management: the Sun Tzu Way" program, he is also Country Manager and Director of Adia Personnel Services Pte. Ltd. in Singapore, a member of the Swiss-based Adia International which operates over 1,900 offices worldwide to provide innovative and creative staffing solutions for clients.

His other books include *Sun Tzu & Management, Sun Tzu's Art of War, Personnel Management Manual, Personnel Policies* and *Applying Sun Tzu's Art of War in Corporate Politics.*

INTRODUCTION

When Sun Tzu, a native of Qi, wrote the *Art of War* some 2,500 years ago, He Lu, the Prince of Wu at that time, was so impressed by what he read that he granted him an audience.

Prince He Lu, who had read all of Sun Tzu's thirteen chapters on warfare, wanted to test Sun Tzu's skill in drilling troops, using women. Sun Tzu was prepared to face this challenge and Prince He Lu sent for 180 ladies from his palace.

Sun Tzu divided them into two companies, each headed by one of the Prince's two favourite concubines. After arming all the women with spears, Sun Tzu asked: "Do you know what is front and back, right and left?"

When all the women replied in the affirmative, Sun Tzu went on to instruct them thus: "When I command 'front,' you must face directly ahead; 'turn left,' you must face to your left; 'turn right,' you must face to your right; 'back,' you must turn right around towards your back."

As all the women assented, Sun Tzu laid out the executioner's weapons to show his seriousness on discipline and began the drill to the sounds of drumbeats and shouts of commands. None of the women moved. Instead, they burst into laughter.

Sun Tzu patiently told them that commands which are unclear and, therefore, not thoroughly understood would be the commander's fault, and proceeded to instruct them once more.

When the drums were beaten a second time and the commands repeated, the women again burst into fits of laughter. This time Sun Tzu said: "Commands which are unclear and not thoroughly understood would be the commander's fault. But when the commands are clear and the soldiers nonetheless do not carry them out, then it is the fault of their officers." So saying, he ordered both the leading concubines out for execution.

The Prince, who was witnessing the drill from a raised pavilion, on seeing his favourite concubines being sent out for execution, was greatly alarmed and quickly sent an aide to Sun Tzu with the message: "I believe the general is capable of drilling troops. Without these two concubines, my food and drink will be tasteless. It is my desire that they be spared."

Sun Tzu replied that having received the royal commission to lead the troops in the field, he can disregard any of the Ruler's commands as he sees fit. Accordingly, he had the two concubines beheaded as an example and thereafter appointed two women next in line to replace the executed ones as company leaders.

Subsequently, the drill proceeded smoothly with every woman turning left, right, front or back; kneeling or rising, with perfect accuracy and precision, without uttering any dissent.

Sun Tzu then sent a messenger to the Prince requesting him to inspect the troops which he declared as having been properly drilled and disciplined, and prepared even to go through fire and water for the Prince.

When the Prince declined, Sun Tzu remarked: "The Prince is only fond of words which he cannot put into practice."

Greatly ashamed by what he heard, and recognising Sun Tzu's ability, Prince He Lu promptly appointed Sun Tzu as the supreme commander of the Wu armies.

From 506BC, Sun Tzu led five expeditions against the State of Chu which had regarded Wu as a vassal. He defeated the armies of Chu and forced his way into the

Introduction

Chu capital, Ying-du, while King Zhao fled leaving his country on the verge of extermination.

For almost twenty years thereafter, the armies of Wu continued to be victorious against those of its neighbours, the States of Qi, Qin and Yue. However, after Sun Tzu's death, his successors failed to follow his precepts and suffered defeat after defeat until 473BC when the kingdom became extinct.

"If the slight cannot be tolerated, the big scheme will be upset."

— *Ssuma I*
*(Warlord of Three Kingdoms Period,
AD220 to AD280)*

PART I

Applying The Art Of War

Memorandum 1

To : All Managers
From : General Manager's Office

Beginning today, I will from time to time share with you the philosophy of a 500BC master strategist, Sun Tzu, who wrote the book called *Art Of War*. You will in time understand how wise his words are which can be applied to managing your staff and tackling business problems and competitors:

> "The art of war is of vital importance to the state; the way of life or death; the road to safety or ruin. It is essential that it is studied. Therefore, appraise it in terms of the five fundamental factors and compare the seven elements later named – so that you may assess its importance. The first of these factors is the moral law; the second, heaven; the third, earth; the fourth, command; and the fifth, doctrine. By moral law, I mean that which causes the people to be in total accord with their ruler, so that they will follow him in life and unto death without fear for their lives and undaunted by any peril."
>
> *– Sun Tzu*

From the above, we should look on our daily management effort as a sort of warfare, that is, a serious exercise and not something to be treated lightly. In recognising the importance of human resource, we must first manage our staff well so as to motivate them to excel in commitment and productivity to solve our business problems and do better than our competitors. When we treat people with respect and fairness, they will reciprocate in turn. This is the essence of the moral law. Encourage team spirit, be firm yet fair.

War At Work

Memorandum 2

To : All Managers
From : General Manager's Office

Last week, I mentioned the five fundamental factors named by Sun Tzu: moral law, heaven, earth, command and doctrine. I have explained moral law. Today, let us look at heaven and earth:

> "By heaven, I mean the working of natural forces; the effects of winter's cold and summer's heat, and the conduct of military operations according to the seasons. By earth, I mean whether the distances are great or short, whether the ground is easy or difficult to travel on, whether it is open ground or narrow passes, and the chances of life or death."
>
> *– Sun Tzu*

In the modern context, heaven can be taken to mean climate, that is, an organisation's climate – a warm, cohesive and happy environment in an organisation as opposed to a cold, fragmented and gloomy one. Thus, work towards improving the climate in our own organisation so that our staff can be motivated towards happily racing ahead of our competitors at any time. As for Sun Tzu's treatise on earth, I interpret it to mean knowledge of the terrain, that is, the resources available to us, limitations and the environmental factors (such as market demand, pricing, special norms, technological changes, legislation, etc.) affecting both ourselves and our competitors. Such knowledge is most important and ought to be studied carefully if we wish to make sound business decisions. One word of caution though – do not overstudy and end up making a decision which is long past its time and application!

Memorandum 3

To : All Managers
From : General Manager's Office

This week, let us look at Sun Tzu's fourth fundamental factor – command:

"By command, I mean the general's stand for the virtues of wisdom, sincerity, benevolence, courage and strictness."

– *Sun Tzu*

If we are wise, we can recognise changing circumstances and thus act accordingly. If sincere, our staff can be certain of the way rewards and punishment are given. If benevolent, we are seen to care for employees, sympathise with them, and appreciate their effort and toil. If courageous, we are not hesitant in making decisions to seize the opportunity. If strict, our staff are disciplined because they realise we will not hesitate to punish.

Memorandum 4

To : All Managers
From : General Manager's Office

It has been some time since I last shared with you the philosophy of the master strategist Sun Tzu. For the new managers and also to refresh the memories of the incumbents, I herewith append copies of my earlier memos for all concerned to read. Today, I shall touch upon Sun Tzu's fifth fundamental factor – doctrine:

> "By doctrine, I mean the way the army is organised in its proper sub-divisions, the gradations of ranks among the officers, the maintenance of supply routes and the control of provisioning for the army."
>
> – *Sun Tzu*

As you can see, management concepts like hierarchy as depicted in organisation charts, and functions of planning, organising, directing and controlling, were already in existence in China some 2,500 years ago. In essence, I believe Sun Tzu's stand so far (as per the five fundamental factors) points towards self-development and consolidation of one's own resources first before entertaining any thought of competing successfully. We must first organise ourselves within a systematic and efficient environment before we can ever dream of doing better than our competitors. Let us start soonest in organising ourselves to create a more systematic and efficient environment for productive work!

Memorandum 5

To : All Managers
From : General Manager's Office

Having examined the five fundamental factors espoused by Sun Tzu, let us now look at his summation and comparison of the seven elements:

"There is no general who is unfamiliar with these five matters. Those who master them will win; those who do not will fail. Therefore, when laying your plans, compare the following elements, appraising them carefully: Which ruler possesses the moral law; whose commander is the most capable; which army obtains the advantages of heaven and the earth; on which side are regulations and instructions carried out better; which army is the stronger; which has the better trained officers and men; and in which army is there certainty of rewards and punishments being dispensed; I will be able to forecast which side will be victorious and which defeated."

– Sun Tzu

Everything depends on how well we know our objectives, the circumstances, the resources available to us, the limitations we are subject to, and similarly those faced by our competitors. To put it simply, in Sun Tzu's own words: "Know yourself, know your enemy, one hundred battles, one hundred victories." We should therefore make it a habit to undertake a thorough SWOT (Strengths-Weaknesses-Opportunities-Threats) analysis before embarking on any project.

War At Work

Memorandum 6

To : All Managers
From : General Manager's Office

Have you applied Sun Tzu's five fundamentals and seven elements yet? If so, then you have consolidated your position, that is know your objectives, the circumstances, the resources available to you, the limitations you are subject to, and similarly know those faced by your competitors. Thence, it is now time to know more about warfare:

> "All warfare is based on deception. Therefore, when capable, pretend to be incapable; when active, inactive; when near, make the enemy believe that you are far away; when far away, that you are near. Hold out baits to lure the enemy; feign disorder and strike him. When he has the advantageous position, prepare against him; when he is strong, avoid him. If he is prone to choleric temper, irritate him. Pretend weakness so that he may become arrogant. If he is at ease, put him under a strain to wear him down. When his forces are united, divide them. Attack where he is unprepared; appear where you are not expected."
>
> – *Sun Tzu*

In short, do the unexpected and pursue the indirect approach in order to catch our competitors off-guard. Never allow our behaviour to become predictable but seek to anticipate those of our competitors. And to do these things, we must again go by the very maxim: "Know yourself, know your enemy, one hundred battles, one hundred victories." For example, if someone we are negotiating with, is expecting toughness on our part, an insignificant concession given by us at the very start could very well disarm him and pave the way for a more conducive and mutually beneficial negotiation. Conversely, if others think that they can simply walk over us, then their complacency should be jolted by our taking on a tougher stand, for example, the more someone thinks we are interested in his offer, the more we will go all out to appear that we are not.

War At Work

Memorandum 7

To : All Managers
From : General Manager's Office

By Sun Tzu's calculations, even in 500BC warfare can be an extremely expensive affair – to raise a hundred thousand troops may amount to thousands of gold pieces a day! He thus cautions against prolonged warfare:

> "Victory is the main object in war. If this is long delayed, weapons are blunted and the ardour of the soldiers will be dampened. When troops attack cities, their strength will be exhausted, and if the campaign is protracted, the resources of the state will not be enough to outlast the strain. When your weapons are dulled, your ardour dampened, your strength exhausted and treasure spent, other rulers will take advantage of your extremity to act. And then no man, however wise, will be able to avert the inevitable that follows. Thus, while we have heard of stupid haste in war, we have not yet seen a clever operation that was prolonged. History has shown that there has never been a country benefitting from prolonged warfare."
>
> – *Sun Tzu*

Thus, do not take warfare lightly lest it becomes too costly. Cost here can take more forms than finances alone. For example, a wrong decision could also cost us our reputation or position. Thus, never wage a war unless we have planned seriously for it and are sure of a quick victory! A cost-and-benefit analysis should be done before making a decision to take on any of our competitors. Here, the maxim "know yourself, know your enemy, one hundred battles, one hundred victories" applies even more aptly.

Memorandum 8

To : All Managers
From : General Manager's Office

Again, let us read some extracts of Sun Tzu's treatise on warfare:

"The skilful general neither requires a second levy of conscripts nor more than one provisioning. They carry war materials from the homeland, but forage on the enemy. Thus, the army is plentifully provided with food. When the treasury is impoverished, it is because military operations are being maintained from a distance; carriage of supplies for great distances renders the people destitute... Hence the wise general sees to it that his troops feed on the enemy, for one cartload of the enemy's provisions is equivalent to twenty of his; one picul of enemy fodder to twenty from one's own store."

– Sun Tzu

Always attempt to do it right the first time! If not, learn a lesson and do it right at least the second time – too many repetitions are wasteful, considering the costs involved. In Sun Tzu's time, transportation over long distances was a burden on manpower and finance – that is why he advocates feeding on the enemy. In today's context, for any project we undertake, see if we can get others to sponsor, that is, finance it. If we are both cunning and skilful in our planning and marketing of the project, it will not be too difficult to find sponsors for mutual gain.

Memorandum 9

To : All Managers
From : General Manager's Office

Sun Tzu concludes his chapter on 'Waging War' by saying:

"Be kind towards captives and care for them. This is called 'using the captured foe to strengthen one's own force.' In war, what matters is victory, not prolonged campaigns. And therefore the general who understands war is the arbiter of the people's fate and on him depends whether the nation shall be at peace or in danger."

– *Sun Tzu*

During Sun Tzu's time, men and weapons were seen as essential war resources. Captives, if shown kindness by their host, can be 'turned around' to fight against their former lords. In today's application, always remember we are in business and hence do not be too personal. If a deal does not work out as we wish, harbour no grievance or enmity towards our counterpart in the negotiation. Continue niceties for who knows, that person may give us the advantage in some other future deals. Do not waste time over lost deals; be swift in changing tactics and move on to score other victories.

Applying The *Art Of War*

Memorandum 10
To : All Managers
From : General Manager's Office

Now that we have seen Sun Tzu's chapter on 'Waging War,' let us look next at his essay on 'Offensive Strategy' which he starts by saying:

"Fighting to win one hundred victories in one hundred battles is not the supreme skill. To break the enemy's resistance without fighting is the supreme skill. Generally, in war the best policy is to take the enemy's country whole and intact; to ruin it is not so good. Also, it is better to capture the enemy's army than to destroy it; to take intact a regiment, a company or a five-man squad is better than to destroy them."

— Sun Tzu

Yes, why be destructive? Can you imagine a corporate raider using tactics which would mortally damage the company he wishes to take over? What is the point? As for the ultimate skill of subduing an enemy without actual fighting, this is certainly an advancement on the maxim of "know yourself, know your enemy, one hundred battles, one hundred victories". It is deep but recall what I have said previously – we are in business. So, why show a negative hand and destroy whatever future advantage we may have? A subtle approach may sometimes prove better than direct confrontation.

13

Memorandum 11

To : All Managers
From : General Manager's Office

On Sun Tzu's 'Offensive Strategy,' we learn that 'to break the enemy's resistance without fighting is the supreme skill.' Let us now see how this can be done:

"Thus, the general skilled in war places priority in attacking the enemy's strategy; the next best is to disrupt any alliances of the enemy."

– Sun Tzu

Attacking the enemy's strategy calls for foresight and advance preparation. This means the ability to conceptualise problems well in advance and to resolve them before they arise. Get to know and attack a competitor's plans at the inception stage. Do not wait for a threat to materialise. Advance knowledge is thus important. And of course, be fast to act. In the case of disrupting an enemy's alliances, it simply means never allowing any competitor to team up against us. Look into ways and means of severing and dissolving such alliances.

Memorandum 12

To : All Managers
From : General Manager's Office

Sun Tzu's 'Offensive Strategy' went on to caution:
"The worst policy of all is to attack walled cities."

– *Sun Tzu*

As I see it, a 'city' in today's context is something which can be related to a competitor (examples include a company's name, building, product, etc.) We should avoid bad-mouthing another company or its products, even though the company or products may belong to our competitor. It is not only unprofessional and unethical but would only result in ourselves reflected as being unduly envious or incapable of meeting competition head-on. If we have to attack a competitor, do so subtly.

War At Work

Memorandum 13

To : All Managers
From : General Manager's Office

This week, I would like to repeat Sun Tzu's call to break the enemy's resistance without fighting. The master strategist himself sums it up as follows:

> "The skilful general subdues the enemy's army without fighting. He captures cities without laying siege to them and overthrows the enemy's reign without protracted operations. Aim to take All-under-Heaven intact. Thus your troops are not wornout and your gains will be complete. This offensive strategy is that of using the sheathed sword."
>
> – *Sun Tzu*

If this philosophy sounds impossible and too far-fetched, think again. Always bear in mind that we are in business to satisfy customers and make profits. It is inevitable to have competitors but if we are going to spend all our energy and resources battling our competitors to the point of destroying them totally, what is there left for us? What good shall be derived from such intense fighting? Besides, public sentiment often goes to the 'underdog' and a victory resulting in destruction of our competitors would not really serve us well.

Memorandum 14

To : All Managers
From : General Manager's Office

The struggle for supremacy in the business 'battlefields' can often be fierce and risky. One must always be flexible and know when to fight and when not to:

> "When our casualties increase, then withdraw. If our force is so much weaker than our enemy's, we should avoid him; for if a small army is stubborn, it will only end up being captured by the larger enemy force."
>
> – *Sun Tzu*

As the saying goes: "He who runs away lives to fight another day." One survives by being prudent rather than being stubborn. The ability to manage change and to ensure continuity through a period of change is becoming more and more necessary. A company may have invested so much in a particular project that its management is unwilling to face reality when the investment is unsuccessful. Believing it has 'invested too much to quit,' the company may carry on throwing in good money even after a venture has turned bad. In such cases, it may be necessary to dispose of (thus cutting losses) the unsuccessful project and reinvest the proceeds elsewhere rather than stubbornly clinging on to it and sinking deeper into the red. Similarly, there are times when it is better to avoid a 'fight' with an aggressive (and stronger) competitor.

War At Work

Memorandum 15

To : All Managers
From : General Manager's Office

The Japanese Air Force bombed Pearl Harbour exactly 48 years ago, catching the U.S. forces off-guard. It is thus quite apt to share more of Sun Tzu's thoughts on 'Offensive Strategy' with you on this day:

> "There are three ways whereby a ruler can bring misfortune upon his army: By commanding an army to advance or retreat, when ignorant of whether to advance or retreat. This is called 'hobbling the army.' By trying to administer an army the same way he administers a kingdom, when ignorant of military affairs. This causes the officers to be perplexed. By using the army officers without discrimination, when ignorant of the military principle of being flexible with circumstances. This causes doubts in the minds of the officers. When the army is confused and suspicious, neighbouring rulers will surely cause trouble."
>
> *— Sun Tzu*

Ignorance is indeed terrible. Thus, we must strive to know our job well, in order to make effective decisions. While staff managers may go by set procedures to get things done, line managers may have to resort to expediency and flexibility. Hence, those assigned to do a job for which he or she has the necessary knowledge and ability, should be allowed to get on with as little interference as possible. Interference by anyone else will only lead to confusion since there will be no unity of command. Confusion will only result in chaos and the subsequent collapse of the organisation.

Memorandum 16

To : All Managers
From : General Manager's Office

Having seen how terrible ignorance and interference can be, we shall now look at how one can use knowledge to become victorious:

"Thus we may know there are five circumstances in which victory may be predicted: He who knows when he can fight and when not to fight will be victorious. He who understands the use of both large and small forces will win. He whose ranks are united in purpose will be victorious. He who is prepared and lies in wait for an enemy who is not, will be victorious. He who has capable generals and without interference by the ruler will be victorious. It is in these five matters that the way to victory is known. Therefore I say: 'If you know yourself and know your enemy; in a hundred battles you will never fear the result. When you know yourself but not your enemy, your chances of winning or losing are equal. If you know neither yourself nor your enemy, you will certainly be in danger in every battle.'"

– Sun Tzu

Again we are reminded of Sun Tzu's maxim: "Know yourself, know your enemy, one hundred battles, one hundred victories." Knowledge is power. With knowledge, not only is one able to manipulate circumstances to become victorious but also to build harmony in human relationships. Knowledge also enables one to prepare beforehand to face any contingency. It is again with knowledge that one would be able to earn the trust and confidence of one's superiors so as to be allowed to work with as little interference as possible.

War At Work

Memorandum 17

To : All Managers
From : General Manager's Office

Seeing that this is the final day of the year, let me ask all of you to reflect on the year that has gone by. I hope you have taken Sun Tzu's writings as shared with you over the past seven months to heart. With such reflections, it is appropriate for us to go into Sun Tzu's opening lines on 'Tactics':

> "Skilful warriors of ancient times first sought for themselves an invincible position whereby they will await the opportunity to strike at their enemy's vulnerability. Invincibility lies in one's own hands but the enemy's vulnerability is of his own making. Thus, those skilled in war can make themselves invincible but the enemy's vulnerability is provided only by the enemy himself. Therefore one may know how to win and yet is unable to do it. To be invincible, use defensive tactics; to make the enemy vulnerable, go on the offensive. Defend when one's strength is insufficient; attack when abundant."
>
> *– Sun Tzu*

What Sun Tzu mean here is that we should practice tolerance so as to secure our own position well and bid our time for our competitors to make mistakes. Do not be hasty in making decisions when unsure of our position but once we are certain of the resources available to us, go all out to seize opportunities. For example, make sure we have the plans ready, manpower on standby, financing arranged before making an aggressive entry into a competitor's market. If our competitors are not prepared, their weaknesses will surely surface.

Memorandum 18

To : All Managers
From : General Manager's Office

Happy New Year, everyone. I hope your New Year resolutions include the mastery of Sun Tzu's *Art of War* for greater efficiency and effectiveness at work. Let us continue with his lesson on 'Tactics':

"To foresee a victory that others can also foresee is no great feat. There is no greatness in winning battles and being proclaimed universally as an expert, for to lift a rabbit's hair requires no great strength; to see the sun and moon is no sign of sharp sight; to hear the thunderclap is no sign of sharp hearing. What the ancients called a skilful fighter is one who not only wins but wins with ease. But the victories shall neither earn him reputation for wisdom nor credit for valour. For victories are such, they are gained in circumstances that have not been revealed and he thus wins no reputation for wisdom; and as the enemy submits without bloodshed, he receives no credit for valour. He wins by making no mistakes. Making no mistakes means already having established the certainty of victory; conquering an enemy who is already defeated. Therefore, a skilful commander puts himself in a position secured against defeat and misses no opportunity to defeat his enemy. In this way, the victorious army seeks battle only after the victory has been secured; an army destined to defeat fights in the hope of winning."

– Sun Tzu

Quite a mouthful to swallow, but exceedingly meaningful. I believe this is Sun Tzu's attempt to teach humility to the victorious general. Do not boast how clever or brave we are, for true cleverness or bravery should be concealed lest our competitors discover our plans and capability. Make arrangements quietly to secure our victory and only then announce our intention. For example, plan quietly and make inroads into our competitor's market first before announcing in public our intention to be the market leader.

Author's Footnote: This book should not have been published at all if I were to go strictly by Sun Tzu's teachings, that is, if I had wanted to be a formidable force in the business world, then I should quietly and surely go about my job without sharing my hard-earned experience with everyone out there who may someday do 'battle' with me!

Memorandum 19

To : All Managers
From : General Manager's Office

Apart from being humble (as mentioned in my last memo), we should also practise self-discipline:

> "The good commander seeks virtues and goes about disciplining himself according to the laws so as to effect control over his success."
>
> *– Sun Tzu*

There are countless gifted executives who simply lack the necessary initiative to put their ideas, convictions and dreams into practice. So, it is not good enough claiming we have ambitions if in the end we fail to take any action to realise these ambitions. Much effort and sacrifice would be demanded because a manager can only develop success by first developing himself or herself. Self-discipline is hence essential if we are to break from the easier albeit non-productive routines of hesitating to do something (claiming "heck, it's impossible!"), procrastinating on something which ought to be done immediately ("there's always tomorrow"), or waiting for someone else to take the lead ("let us wait and see"), etc. Start practising self-discipline now by working on that tedious task (whatever it may be) which you have been procrastinating out of dread or plain laziness.

War At Work

Memorandum 20

To : All Managers
From : General Manager's Office

Seeing that it is still early in the New Year, let us turn to Sun Tzu's chapter on 'Energy' and see what we can learn about harnessing our energy for a concerted drive towards our objective:

"Management of many is the same as management of a few. It is a matter of dividing up their numbers and functions. Manoeuvering a large army is no different from manoeuvering a small one: it is a matter of formations and signals. In making sure the army can sustain the enemy's attack without suffering defeat, use direct and indirect manoeuvres. Generally, in battle, use the direct methods to engage the enemy forces; indirect methods however are needed to secure victory."

– *Sun Tzu*

We find that the management principles of organising and directing as taught in today's management schools are no different from those applied in ancient times. Sun Tzu also realised in his time that both direct and indirect methods need to be used to achieve one's objective. For example, besides submitting a written proposal to a business party and subsequently talking to persuade his commitment (the direct method), we may even have to talk to those persons close to him with the aim of harnessing their influence to wrap up the deal (the indirect method).

Applying The Art Of War

Memorandum 21

To : All Managers
From : General Manager's Office

Let us continue to see what Sun Tzu has to say about direct and indirect manoeuvering:

"In battle, there are only the direct or indirect methods of fighting but they give an endless combination of manoeuvres. For both forces are interlocked and using one will lead to the other; it is like moving in a circle – you can never come to an end. Who can determine where one ends and the other begins? Torrential water tosses stones along its course due to its momentum. The well-timed swoop of a hawk enables it to strike its prey. Therefore, the momentum of one who is skilled in war will be overwhelming and his decision to strike must be well-timed. Energy is like a fully-drawn crossbow; the decision to strike is the timely release of the trigger."

– Sun Tzu

Flexibility is essential when using either the direct or indirect approach or even both at the same time. Whichever method is used must depend on the situation. Each situation must be analysed carefully to determine the significant variables involved before making a decision, which when made ought to be swiftly and timely carried out. And again, changing situations may call for changing methods. What is applicable yesterday may no longer apply today!

Memorandum 22

To : All Managers
From : General Manager's Office

After touching on the direct and indirect methods of fighting in his essay on 'Energy,' Sun Tzu went on to describe a battle situation with emphasis on the need for deceitful appearance:

> "Amid the turmoil and uproar of battle, the situation may appear to be chaotic and yet no real chaos exists; troops seem to be in disarray and yet cannot be routed. What is seen as confusion is actually good order; appearance of fear is in reality courage; appearance of weakness is yet true strength. Order or disorder depends on organisation; concealing valour for a cowardly front is on circumstances; masking strength with weakness is to be effected by tactical disposition. Thus, the skilful general keeps the enemy on the move by maintaining deceitful appearances; he holds out something that the enemy is certain to grab at, and with such baits keep the enemy going to where he lies in wait to strike. A skilled commander conserves energy from the situation instead of wasting his men. He selects his men according to their talents and uses them to exploit the situation."
>
> *– Sun Tzu*

Again we are reminded of the limitless use of deceit to create situations where we can, apart from misleading our competitors, further lead them where we want them to be. Here, it is also beneficial to learn from Sun Tzu, the proper utilisation of personnel. Understand the strengths and weaknesses of each member of our staff so that we can make the best use of each individual for any given situation we have planned.

Memorandum 23

To   :   All Managers
From :   General Manager's Office

Sun Tzu's opening sentence in his essay on 'Weak and Strong Points' says:

"The one who is first to occupy the battlefield to await the enemy will be fresh and at ease; he who comes later to rush into the fight will be exhausted. Therefore, the skilful commander imposes his will on the enemy by making the enemy come to him instead of being brought to the enemy. To do this, he offers the enemy some advantages; and similarly, he is able to prevent the enemy's coming by inflicting damage on the enemy. When the enemy is taking his ease, harass him; when well-supplied with food, attack his supply lines to starve him out; when he is at rest, force him to move. Appear at those places that he must hasten to defend; move swiftly to those places where you are not expected."

– *Sun Tzu*

Now you may perhaps understand why I have always been harping on the need to be early for appointments or meetings. When we make it a point to be early, we tend to be better prepared for the occasion. Such preparation will usually provide us the necessary knowledge and confidence to impose control on the situation. When we are in control, it is relatively easier for us to see what is happening, or about to happen, in order to 'call the shots'.

Memorandum 24

To : All Managers
From : General Manager's Office

The Chinese New Year is just round the corner and I seem to detect a certain 'holiday mood' in the air. Do not ever make the mistake of being complacent – our competitors may just be about to hit us for all we know. Even if they are not, never relax our guard for as Sun Tzu says:

> "That you may march a thousand *li* without exhaustion is due to the country being free of enemy troops. You can be sure of taking what you attack if you attack those places which are undefended. To ensure the safety of your position, hold only those positions that cannot be attacked. For a general who is skilled in the offensive, the enemy would not know what to defend; and for one who is skilful in the defensive, the enemy would not know what to attack. Subtle and secretive, the skilled learns to be invisible and silent to control the enemy's fate. He whose advance cannot be resisted makes for the enemy's weak areas; if need to withdraw, he moves so swiftly that he cannot be overtaken."
>
> *– Sun Tzu*

As I have said earlier, never be complacent. While it is all right to make our competitor see our strengths as weaknesses, it is certainly not all right if we become complacent by failing to cause his strengths to become weaknesses or finding out where he is weak. Even if we are not taking any offensive action, it is still useful to try finding out how our competitor is doing or what he is up to.

Memorandum 25

To : All Managers
From : General Manager's Office

Last week, I cautioned you against complacency. Instead of wasting time on idle pursuits, make good use of your time to learn more about our competitors and to explore how we can race ahead of them:

> "When I wish to fight, my enemy who may be sheltered by high ramparts and deep moats, can be forced to come out into an engagement if I were to attack a position that he will be obliged to relieve. When I wish to avoid a fight, I can prevent an engagement even though the battlelines had been drawn by diverting my enemy with something odd and unexpected thrown in his way."
>
> *– Sun Tzu*

This means we must always be in control in any situation. To be in control, we must be capable of making decisions which are entirely our own and not subject to any undue influence. Effective decisions can only be made if we are resourceful enough to find out what our competitors' weaknesses and strengths are and understand how to exploit these weaknesses yet wise enough to avoid their strengths. Only then will we be able to cause our competitors to act as we would want them to.

War At Work

Memorandum 26

To : All Managers
From : General Manager's Office

It is very necessary to thoroughly know our competitors for in his essay on 'Strong and Weak Points,' Sun Tzu elaborates this need as follows:

> "By discovering my enemy's disposition and at the same time concealing mine from him, I can concentrate my forces while he must divide his. Knowing his dispositions, I can use my total strength against a part of his. If he is ignorant of mine, he will have to spread out his forces to defend every point. This will give me superiority in numbers. And if I were to use my superior strength to attack an inferior one, those I deal with will be in dire straits. The enemy must not know where I intend to attack. For if he knows not, he must prepare for possible attack in many places; and in such preparation, his forces shall be so spread out that those I have to fight at any given point will be few."
>
> *– Sun Tzu*

Once we know what our competitors are up to, and without their knowing what we are up to, we will be in a superior position to control the situation. This way, our customers' base may be expanded or our penetration into the competitors' market may be made without alerting them and thus take preventive measures against us; and our promotions may be rated more attractive and thus favourably publicised without having the ideas stolen and limelight taken away from our efforts.

Memorandum 27

To : All Managers
From : General Manager's Office

Over the weekend, I reflected upon Sun Tzu's insistence on knowing what our competitors are doing while preventing them from knowing what we are up to. He has this to say:

> "One who has few must prepare for defence; one who has many shall make the enemy prepare for defence...Thus, I can create victory. Even if the enemy is numerous, I can prevent him from fighting. Find out his plans to know which of his strategies will be successful and which will not. Provoke to agitate him and so learn the pattern of his movements. Force him to show his disposition and thus ascertaining his strengths and weaknesses."
>
> *– Sun Tzu*

Again we are advised on the necessity of knowledge. It does not matter if our competitors are bigger than we are. We can still be in control if we know more about their plans to determine the strengths and weaknesses of their strategies. Given that man is a most egoistic creature and often prone to being emotional, it is not that difficult to get him to talk. You may be surprised how easily people can be provoked into talking. Be alert and listen attentively (do not also join in talking) when they start 'shooting off'. Remember, you can use whatever you have learned from those who cannot keep their mouth shut only if they do not learn anything from you!

Memorandum 28

To : All Managers
From : General Manager's Office

While it is all right to know our competitors' activities, it is certainly not all right for them to know ours. In his essay on 'Weak and Strong Points,' Sun Tzu goes on to say:

> "The supreme skill in commanding troops is in the shapeless command. Then the prying of the subtlest spies cannot penetrate for the laying of plans against you. The shapes I take shall lay plans for victory but such are beyond the comprehension of the masses. While all can see the external aspects, none can understand the way I scored my victory. Thus when I win a victory, I do not repeat the tactics but respond to circumstances in limitless ways. Military tactics are similar to water, for just as flowing water runs away from high places and speeds downwards, so an army avoids the strong enemy and strikes at the weak one. As water shapes its flow according to the ground, an army wins by relating to the enemy it faces. And just as water retains no constant shape, in war there shall be no constant conditions. Thus, the one who can modify his tactics according to the enemy's situations shall be victorious and may be called The Divine Commander."
>
> *– Sun Tzu*

Without a doubt, while seeking information about our competitors, we must never let ours be known. Keep quiet and be alert to situations which may cause leakage of information. For example, do not talk business in lifts or while being chauffeur-driven. Do not become predictable. Change your tactics. Practise flexibility in view of today's fight for corporate and business survival and the growth taking place in a fast changing environment of new and knowledgeable competitors, new technologies and volatile political conditions. One wins through knowledge of such matters and thoughtful planning to stay on top of current problems. Search relentlessly for and study all information.

War At Work

Memorandum 29

To : All Managers
From : General Manager's Office

This week we shall go to Sun Tzu's chapter on 'Manoeuvres' which he opens by saying:

> "Without harmony in the State, no military expedition can be made; without harmony in the army, no battle formation can be directed. In war, the general first receives his commands from the ruler. He then assembles his troops and blends them into a harmonious entity before pitching camp."
>
> – Sun Tzu

Earlier, when I shared Sun Tzu's fifth fundamental factor on doctrine with you, I said that we must first organise ourselves within a systematic and efficient environment before we can ever dream of outdoing our competitors. At this point, we are again reminded of the need to establish harmony within our organisation prior to making any move against our competitors. Staff morale must be high and commitment towards productivity must be obtained. Only then can we move for market expansion or strive for corporate leadership. As managers, you are entrusted with this task of building staff morale and commitment in your respective departments. You can do this by being firm yet fair. Firmness ensures high standards of work and determination to do a job well. Fairness ensures the equitable dispensing of rewards and punishments.

Memorandum 30

To : All Managers
From : General Manager's Office

On 'Manoeuvres,' Sun Tzu says:

"Nothing is more difficult than directing manoeuvres. The difficulty lies in turning the devious into the direct, and misfortune into gain. Thus, adopt an indirect route and divert the enemy by enticing him with a bait. Once done, you may march forth after he has gone and arrive before him. One who is able to do this knows the strategy of the direct and indirect."

– Sun Tzu

Sometimes, we may have no choice but to put on masks and act out 'shows' to conceal our objectives from our competitors, satisfy our customers, or placate our staff. For example, an important but fussy customer may believe that a receptionist was rude to him and accordingly demands that disciplinary action be taken against that receptionist. The receptionist who has a good track record for being courteous and efficient could have been taken ill on that particularly hectic day. We want to lose neither customer nor receptionist. Thus, we may have to put on a 'show' for the customer that the receptionist will be thoroughly disciplined but in reality no serious action is taken apart from constructive counselling. We should have no qualms about putting on masks and acting out 'shows'. Always remember, worrying will only make problems worse; view problems as challenges and you may yet turn vulnerability into a great advantage. It is difficult but not impossible.

Memorandum 31

To : All Managers
From : General Manager's Office

While Sun Tzu talks about several dangers in 'Manoeuvres,' there is one in particular I wish to highlight:

> "When one sets in motion an entire army to chase an advantage, the chances are that he will not attain it."
>
> *– Sun Tzu*

We must try to set the right values in all that we do. Know that nothing is more important than our men because it is through them that we can turn out products or provide services. Thence do not waste their time or efforts. If we understand values, then we will know what is essential and what is not before calling for meetings which can always take up a great deal of time. Thus, to solve minor problems, there is really no need to call a meeting of every manager or executive. Neither is it necessary for everyone to be personally present for functions and/or discussions.

Memorandum 32

To : All Managers
From : General Manager's Office

To continue with Sun Tzu's essay on 'Manoeuvres,' the great strategist says:

> "War is based on deception. Move only if there is a real advantage to be gained and create changes in the situation by dividing or concentrating your forces. Be swift as the wind, compact as the forest. In raiding and plundering, like fire; in stability, as the mountain. Let your plans be unfathomable as the clouds and move like the thunderbolt."
>
> *– Sun Tzu*

Wearing all sorts of masks to act out 'shows' can be pretty tiring. Thus, avoid total confrontation in business as such situations can result in disastrous consequences if not handled properly. Expand and compete only when victory is certain and the objective is worth the effort. In such cases, we must have sufficient support in terms of information, finance and manpower. Timing is very important and once a decision is made, act with speed and total commitment. Our plans or moves should not be easily understood by our competitors.

Memorandum 33

To : All Managers
From : General Manager's Office

In his essay on 'Manoeuvres,' Sun Tzu also touches somewhat on motivation:

> "When plundering the countryside and having captured new lands, divide the profits among your men...An army may be robbed of its spirit and the commander be robbed of his wits. In the morning, a soldier's spirit is keenness, during the day, it gradually diminishes, and in the evening, the soldier thinks only of returning to camp. Thus, the skilful commander avoids the enemy whose spirit is at its keenness and instead attacks only when the enemy's spirit is sluggish and thinking of camp."
>
> *— Sun Tzu*

Show appreciation to our staff for a job well done. Reward them financially in the form of annual bonuses and/or increments, or noting them for promotions when opportunity arises. Even a smile and a word of praise go a long way to motivate an employee. Encourage staff to report for work early – it not only reflects enthusiasm for work but also results in efficiency and effectiveness. Help them if necessary to arrange their work so that they need not have to stay back for overtime which is usually costly and unproductive. There is nothing more irresponsible than a manager who simply approves his staff's overtime claim just to "encourage" him by "helping him earn something extra." This is not only unproductive but it is also cheating the company.

Memorandum 34

To   : All Managers
From : General Manager's Office

Having read that 'crash-course' on motivation in my last memo, let us keep the momentum going:

> "Prepare ourselves in good order to await a disorderly enemy; in calmness, await a boisterous one. This is control of the mind. Close to the battlefield, wait for the enemy coming from afar: at ease, await a tired enemy; with well-fed troops, await hungry ones. This is control of strength."
>
> — *Sun Tzu*

Once we have motivated our staff and have ensured their commitment to stay and contribute towards the achievement of the organisation's goals, we are in a stronger position to bring about change successfully to improve our effectiveness (doing the right things) and efficiency (doing things right). It is only after we have 'tidied up our own house,' thus consolidating our resources that we can take on our competitors with ease and confidence. Always remember our men are our most valuable asset and hence exercise fairness and sensibility in rewarding and treating them. When they are 'well-fed' both in the physical and mental sense, nothing is impossible.

War At Work

Memorandum 35

To : All Managers
From : General Manager's Office

I have been talking, at times quite glibly, on doing the unexpected and enticing our competitors with baits. But be cautioned:

> "Do not pursue an enemy who pretends to flee. Refrain from attacking troops whose spirit is keen. Do not swallow baits put out by the enemy. Avoid stopping enemy troops on the home march. When surrounding an enemy, leave him an escape route. Do not press an enemy to desperation."
>
> *— Sun Tzu*

Never underestimate our competitors. They too can be as knowledgeable and strong as we are, if not more so. That is why we should always seek to avoid open conflict. Much as we can hurt others, they too can hurt us. Compete fairly but always be wise to unfair tactics. During negotiations, much as we can try to convince the other party, respect his decision once he has made up his mind and refuses to budge. Practise tact and allow the other party to step down gracefully – he will respect us for that. Never drive him up against the wall for he will then have nothing to lose but turn around and fight against us all the way.

Memorandum 36

To : All Managers
From : General Manager's Office

We now come to Sun Tzu's next chapter on 'Tactical Variations,' where he says:

> "A wise general considers both the advantages and disadvantages opened to him. When considering the advantages, he makes his plan feasible; when considering the disadvantages, he finds ways to extricate himself from the difficulties."
>
> *– Sun Tzu*

No one can have everything going his way. In all our ventures, there are bound to be good and bad points. Always do a cost-and-benefit analysis before taking any action. Good planning ensures the maximum use of all advantages and the careful consideration of all disadvantages for the provision of safety measures. If we accept that there is bound to be a mixture of good and bad turns in life, and are yet resourceful enough, we may still find opportunities to turn a disadvantaged position into an advantageous one. But for one who is pessimistic and always quick to bemoan, "It's impossible!", then what is possible may very well turn out to be impossible indeed. Such a person will never be successful in life.

Memorandum 37

To : All Managers
From : General Manager's Office

Today, as we look at a rather harsh passage in Sun Tzu's chapter on 'Tactical Variations,' I must first caution you against being carried away by what you read. None of this, of course, should be taken literally. It is only my belief that as professionals, we should compete fairly albeit we must be wise to unfair tactics:

> "Seek to reduce those hostile neighbouring States by inflicting harm on them. Labour them with constant trifle affairs. Lead them by their noses with superficial offers of advantages."
>
> *– Sun Tzu*

In Sun Tzu's time, inflicting harm to an enemy takes the forms of enticing away his capable staff, encouraging some to turn traitors, weaving intrigues and deceit between the enemy and his supporters, corrupting the morals of the enemy or his followers with gifts of intoxicating drugs or liquors, or lovely women so as to encourage excess and unsettling domestic harmony and official duties, etc. Today, such unscrupulous tactics vary in their usage and many young and promising executives have been led astray by heavy gambling, drugs, wine, women and song into corruption and/or failing in their responsibilities which they have been entrusted. Be very careful of those who would take you to this 'downhill slide'.

Memorandum 38

To   :   All Managers
From : General Manager's Office

Let us see what more on 'Tactical Variations' that Sun Tzu can offer us:

> "It is a principle of war that we do not assume the enemy will not come, but instead we must be prepared for his coming; not to presume he will not attack, but instead to make our own position unassailable."
>
> *— Sun Tzu*

The lesson is never to be complacent. Although it is advisable to avoid aggression on our part, we should also avoid taking our competitors for granted. Always be prepared for any aggressive moves made by our competitors. Meanwhile, during the 'peace' period, use our time wisely to consolidate our own positions. Even though we may not eventually 'go to war', there is no harm in seeking self-development and improving our positions. Indeed a good manager will not be complacent but constantly seek new ideas and improvement on the so-called 'one-best way' of doing things.

War At Work

Memorandum 39

To : All Managers
From : General Manager's Office

Sun Tzu ends his chapter on 'Tactical Variations' by cautioning:

> "There are five dangerous faults which a general should not have in his character. Recklessness, which leads to destruction; cowardice, which ends in capture; a quick temper, which enables you to make him look foolish; delicacy in honour, which causes sensitivity to shame; overly compassionate for his men, which exposes him to worry and harassment. These five faults in a general can seriously ruin military operations."
>
> *– Sun Tzu*

We are reckless when we do not plan well. Good planning calls for the gathering of essential information for a thorough cost-and-benefit analysis. If too cautious, opportunities may escape us and competitors may by then also get to know our plans. Try to curb our temper for we tend to lose control when we are in a rage, thus placing ourselves in a highly vulnerable position for foolish scenes. If too sensitive over our image, we may sometimes become apathetic. Take a cue from top Japanese executives who think nothing shameful in picking up tools and working alongside their mechanics. And while we should care for our men, we should avoid trying to please everyone and end up pleasing no one.

Memorandum 40

To : All Managers
From : General Manager's Office

Sun Tzu's next essay, 'On The March,' gives some invaluable tips on dispensing rewards and punishments:

"When troops are seen whispering amongst themselves in small groups, the general has lost the confidence of his men. Too frequent rewards show that the general is losing control over his men as only rewards can keep them in even temper. Too frequent punishments show him to be in dire distress as nothing else can keep them in check. If the officers at first treat their men harshly and later fear them, the limit of indiscipline is reached."

– Sun Tzu

Does this not remind you of the need to be firm yet fair? As mentioned earlier, firmness ensures high standards of work and determination to do a job well. Fairness ensures the equitable dispensing of rewards and punishments. It is bad policy to reward an employee with salary raises, promotions, bonuses, etc. every now and then as an employee can cease to be motivated thereafter or worse, can come to expect more and more. Similarly, if an employee is punished too often, soon the punishment will lose its effect and the employee might behave even worse. When we start to fear such errant employees, chaos shall reign as mutiny inevitably sets in.

Memorandum 41

To : All Managers
From : General Manager's Office

We have learned not to be complacent in assuming our enemy will kindly spare us from any aggression. What about complacency arising from belief in our own strength?

> "In battle, having more soldiers will not necessarily secure victory. Never advance by relying blindly on the strength of military power. It is sufficient to concentrate our strength, estimate our enemy's position and seek his capture. But anyone who lacks foresight and treats the enemy with contempt and disdain will only end up being captured."
>
> *– Sun Tzu*

Giant corporations have been known to fail simply because their executives became complacent from being overly confident of their strength. It is the classic story of 'the hare and the tortoise' all over again. Even if we have enough resources to start with, we should try not to do everything at once because the many projects may demand too much infusion of time, money and energy and thus causing us to 'overstretch.' And while we can be confident of our 'strength,' never take for granted that a competitor can never catch up with us. Develop our conceptual skill by asking ourselves "What should our organisation be like in the future?"; apply the "What if?" scenarios; and thus work out the appropriate strategies on the basis that competitors could catch up with us the moment we cease to pull our weight.

Memorandum 42

To : All Managers
From : General Manager's Office

From Sun Tzu's essay, 'On The March,' we can also learn how to discipline and control our men:

"Secure the loyalty of your troops first before punishing them or they will not be submissive. When they are loyal and if punishment is not enforced, you still cannot use them. Therefore, treat your men kindly but keep strict control over them to ensure victory. If the commands used in training troops are consistent, soldiers will be disciplined. If not, soldiers are inclined to be disobedient. If a general's commands are consistently credible and obeyed, he enjoys good relationship between him and his men."

– Sun Tzu

If our staff see us as firm yet fair, they are more inclined to obey our instructions. Never practise favouritism as such tends to spoil the favoured worker and demoralise the others. Give consistent instructions to avoid confusion and, hence, disobedience. If we are objective in giving instructions to our staff, a relationship based on trust can be developed between us and our staff, and such shall ensure that instructions are followed readily.

Memorandum 43

To : All Managers
From : General Manager's Office

In his next chapter, 'Terrain,' Sun Tzu touches on responsibility by saying:

> "When troops are inclined to flee, insubordinate against commands, distressed, disorganised, or defeated, it is the fault of the general as none of these calamities arises from natural causes."
>
> *– Sun Tzu*

When things go wrong, it is always tempting to put the blame on others, especially our subordinates. However, remember that as managers, we are responsible for the actions of our staff. Even if we have delegated a job to an employee and he did a bad job, the responsibility is still ours – after all, we picked the wrong man to do the job. Even Sun Tzu knows this principle. The most effective way of preventing mistakes from happening again is to take as much of the blame ourselves as possible and at the same time point them out to our staff. By so doing, not only will we gain the respect of our staff, but they will also learn not to repeat the mistake.

Memorandum 44

To : All Managers
From : General Manager's Office

Earlier this week, I said we should shoulder the responsibility for any mistakes, even if these are made by our staff. Let us now see more of what Sun Tzu has to say on staff control:

> "When the common soldiers are stronger than their officers, they will insubordinate. When the officers are too strong and the troops are weak, the result is collapse. When senior officers are angry and go against orders, and they fight on meeting the enemy without being told by their general whether such is feasible or not, the result is defeat. When the general is morally weak and lacks authority; when his instructions are not clear; when there are no consistent rules to guide both officers and men, and the ranks are slovenly formed, the result is disorganisation."
>
> *– Sun Tzu*

Realise then why we as managers are responsible. To be an effective manager, we must be stronger (in terms of character, knowledge and skills) than our staff in order to be in control. At the same time, we must not only select the staff with the right calibre but we must also develop them to reach our standards of working. Ensure strict control so that none acts out of irrational emotion and against better judgements. We must be seen to be honest, hardworking and decisive. Give clear instructions and provide guidance for efficiency and effectiveness. If we fail in the above, it is no wonder that our staff makes mistakes. Understand now why we are responsible?

Memorandum 45

To : All Managers
From : General Manager's Office

Sun Tzu is quite relentless in reminding us from time to time of his maxim, "know yourself, know your enemy, one hundred battles, one hundred victories":

> "When a general fails to size up his enemy and uses an inferior force to engage a larger one, or weak troops to attack the strong, or neglects to place picked men in the front ranks, the result is a rout."
>
> – *Sun Tzu*

Once again we see how necessary it is to really know our competitors. Nothing is more pathetic than to see a weaker party attempting to take on a stronger one. We must constantly evaluate and compare our position and that of our competitors even though we may not be at 'war.' As information can provide a competitive advantage, we must strive to develop a good management information system. It is also necessary to really know our employees. Recognise each person's strengths but put aside (yet without ignoring) the weaknesses in order to ask ourselves: "What can this man do?" rather than "What can he not do?" Place him in a job where his strengths can be thus utilised to the maximum.

Memorandum 46

To : All Managers
From : General Manager's Office

Sun Tzu has all along been preaching on flexibility to adapt to changes. He says:

> "Conformation of the terrain is the soldier's best ally in battle. Thus, victory rests with the superior general who can size up his enemy and provide for the distances in travel and the nature of the land with all its difficulties. If the situation offers victory but the ruler forbids fighting, the general may still fight. If the situation is such that he cannot win, the general must not fight even if the ruler orders him to do so. Thus, the general who advances without coveting fame and withdraws without fearing disgrace, but whose sole intention is to protect the people and do good service for his ruler, is the precious jewel of the state."
>
> *— Sun Tzu*

We must be quick to change and adapt with circumstances. Get to know our competitors well, assess their strengths and weaknesses as compared to ours, and fully consider the difficulties we face. Above all, never be a 'yes man'. Try to develop our staff as well as ourselves to become independent thinkers. Some of you may have seen me take decisions which may not conform to our bosses' intentions. But you will agree that we have to do so at times if we rightfully believe such is in the best interest of our company.

War At Work

Memorandum 47

To : All Managers
From : General Manager's Office

We have seen how important it is to be knowledgeable. Let us see what more can Sun Tzu offer us in the area of knowledge:

> "If I know my soldiers are capable of attacking the enemy but am unaware that he is invulnerable to attack, my chance of victory is but half. If I know the enemy is open to attack but do not know my soldiers are incapable of attacking him, my chance of victory is but half. If I know he can be attacked and my soldiers are capable of doing it but am unaware that the terrain is unsuited for fighting, I should hold back for my chance of victory is but half. Thus, when those skilled in war make their move, there is no mistake; when they act, they have unlimited resources. So I say: know your enemy, know yourself and your victory will be undoubted. Know Earth and know Heaven and your victory will be complete.
>
> – *Sun Tzu*

Knowledge of having a strong team is still insufficient for business success if we do not realise our competitors' strengths. Similarly, a business venture may fail even if we know our competitors to be weak but do not realise that we are as weak, if not weaker. Even with the knowledge that we are strong and our competitors are weak, failure to grasp the situation may still cause a project to fail. Thus before we act, take every factor into consideration. 'Earth' refers to the ground, which can be interpreted as the situation we are in. 'Heaven' refers to climate, which in today's context, can mean the organisation or political climate. So even if a time comes when we know that we are strong while our competitors are weak, we may still refrain from aggressively penetrating into our competitors' market because it may be a recessionary period where consumers are not spending or the political climate is unstable.

Memorandum 48

To : All Managers
From : General Manager's Office

At this stage, I must remind you that aggression can be very costly for both ourselves and our competitors. But if we are ever threatened, then we must strive to win:

> "Speed is the essence of war. Take advantage of the enemy's lack of preparation; move by using unexpected routes and attack where he has made no defence."
>
> *– Sun Tzu*

While we should try to avoid open confrontation with our competitors, we should constantly find out what they are up to. If we know for sure that any of them is thinking of making aggressive moves into our market, we must move faster by coming up with, and implementing our own counter-measures before the competitor makes his move. For this purpose, it is important to set up and maintain an effective and efficient management information system.

Memorandum 49

To : All Managers
From : General Manager's Office

While information can provide a competitive advantage, staff morale is also essential if we are going to successfully take on our competitors:

> "Give attention to the well-being of your men; do not unnecessarily exhaust them. Keep their spirit united; conserve their energy. Do not let your enemy understand the plans concerning your troops' movement. Put your men in positions where there is no escape and even when facing death, they will not run. In preparing for death, what is there that cannot be achieved? Both officers and men will do their best. In a desperate situation, they lose their sense of fear; without a way out, they shall stand firm. When they are deep within enemy territory they are bound together and without an alternative, they will fight hard. Thus, without need of supervision, they will be alert, and without being asked, they will support their general; without being ordered, they will trust their general. If my officers are not exceedingly rich, it is not that they disdain wealth. If they do not expect long life, it is not due to dislike for longevity."
>
> *– Sun Tzu*

All you need to know about managing people is in the above. Motivation is not just high salary or promise of a lifetime employment alone. Be sensitive to the individual needs of our employees. Start by not overrating our own importance by keeping everything to ourselves. Go ahead and develop our staff by giving them responsibility in their respective areas. You may be surprised how positively most people respond when entrusted with responsibility.

Memorandum 50

To : All Managers
From : General Manager's Office

Sun Tzu, who has also shown himself to be quite critical of a general's character, has advised certain behaviour:

"It is the business of a general to be calm and mysterious; fair and composed. He must be capable of mystifying his officers and men so that they are in ignorance of his true intentions. He forbids the casting of omens and do away with superstitious beliefs that even until the time of death, no calamity need be feared. He changes his arrangements and alters his plans so that no one knows what he is up to. He changes campsites and takes circuitous routes to prevent others from anticipating his purpose. His business is to assemble his troops and throw them into a critical position. He leads them deep into enemy territory to further his plans."

– Sun Tzu

As managers, we must always be seen to be in control for how else can we lead and inspire our staff? While staff should know enough to perform their work well, there are also things they need not have to know. We should thus learn to judge what is confidential and thereafter hold our tongues. Avoid leaving a pattern which can be pieced together by our competitors. Always remember that our business has to improve and expand otherwise it will decline and die. Risks should therefore be taken. We should thus develop our staff and that they are constantly encouraged to seek improvements, to try something new and to take risks. Therefore, do not wet-nurse our staff but train them to thrive under pressure.

Memorandum 51

To : All Managers
From : General Manager's Office

I hope you have digested the contents of yesterday's memo by now. As I am hard-pressed for time, I shall give you another dose as follows:

> "If we cannot fathom the designs of our neighbouring States, we cannot enter into alliances in advance. Those who do not know the conditions of mountains, forests, high and dangerous grounds, defiles, marshes and swamps, cannot conduct the march of an army. Those who do not use local guides cannot benefit from the advantages of the ground."
>
> *– Sun Tzu*

In most industries, firms are mutually dependent, sometimes even complementary. Thus, by entering into an 'alliance' with other firms may offer mutual gains. Estimate what each competitor is likely to do given its history and what is known of its management. Once this is done, we should be able to decide on the strategic factors vital for successful future cooperation or an 'all-out fight.' Do an environmental scanning by seeking information from sources such as the mass media, customers, suppliers, bankers, consultants, superiors, peers, subordinates and personal observation. When we are able to narrow down the subject matter, the source of information should be even more specific. Get the facts from the experts – those who know.

Memorandum 52

To   :   All Managers
From :   General Manager's Office

There are those who insist on defining objectives, formulating policies and everyone must thereafter work according to rules and regulations. There are also those who preach democracy where staff should be allowed to do what they think is necessary. Let us see what Sun Tzu has to say:

> "Bestow rewards without regard to customary rules, issue orders without regard to prescribed procedures. Thus, you may run the entire army as you would one man."
>
> *– Sun Tzu*

While I personally believe in objectives and policies to guide us at work, there are times when circumstances require that one should 'call the shots' without regard to set rules and regulations. As managers we must know and do what is in the best interest of our company. While we should respect the opinions of our staff, remember that decisions are made by us. Never let ourselves be drawn into a general discussion during staff meetings or attempt to please everybody. Hear out the views of others and think what is best for our company, before deciding on the course of action.

Applying The *Art Of War*

Memorandum 53

To : All Managers
From : General Manager's Office

In his essay, 'Attack By Fire,' Sun Tzu again talks about the dangers of war and the need to separate our emotion from the business at hand:

"The enlightened ruler plans well ahead, and good generals serve to execute the plans. Do not act unless it is in the interest of the state. Do not use your troops unless you can win. Do not fight unless you are in danger. No ruler should put troops into the field because he is angry; no general should fight because he is resentful. For an angry man can later become happy, a resentful man become pleased, but a kingdom once destroyed can never be restored nor the dead be brought back to life. Hence the enlightened ruler is prudent and the good general should not be hasty. Thus a country is safe and the army preserved."

– Sun Tzu

Here, Sun Tzu's thoughts are quite consistent with the modern day approach to the functions of directors and their managers – directors govern; the managers manage. Whether as directors or as managers, pay heed to one rule which can be quite difficult to observe: there is no place for emotion in business. As said earlier, open conflict with competitors is best avoided unless we are threatened or there is a great advantage to be gained. To enter into a conflict merely on the account of anger or resentment is not only silly but also highly wasteful.

Memorandum 54
To : All Managers
From : General Manager's Office

We now come to Chapter 13 – also the final chapter – of Sun Tzu's *Art of War* where he gives some sound advice on using spies to get information:

"He who faces an enemy for many years to struggle for the victory that can be decided in a single day and yet remains ignorant of the enemy's position because he begrudges giving ranks, honours and a few hundred pieces of gold, is totally without humanity. Such a man is no leader, no help to his ruler, no master of victory.

The enlightened ruler and the wise general can subdue the enemy whenever they move and they can achieve superhuman feats because they have foreknowledge. This foreknowledge cannot be obtained from spirits, gods, nor by reasoning over past events, nor by calculations. It can only be obtained from men who know the enemy position."

– *Sun Tzu*

Information is extremely vital to any organisation. It gives one the competitive advantage. It may be related to new economic developments, new management techniques, new concepts and ideas. Or we may simply want to find out more about someone whom we wish to do business with or to know what our competitors are up to. Thus, learn to seek information which can be acquired rather cheaply or for free by talking to people, witnessing events, or paying to attend seminars and conferences, reading newspapers, etc. At times we may even have to pay a particular person or group of persons for information. For example, in today's world of corporate intelligence and security, a small coterie of professional firms, the largest worldwide being Kroll Associates, are providing this service.

War At Work

Memorandum 55

To : All Managers
From : General Manager's Office

In his treatise on 'Espionage,' which is his last essay, Sun Tzu reminds:

> "The relationship between the commander and his secret agent is more intimate than all others in the army. The rewards given to secret agents are more liberal than any other given. The confidentiality given to secret operations is greater than for other matters. Only the one who is wise and sagely, benevolent and just, can use secret agents. Only he who is sensitive and subtle can get the truth of their reports. Be subtle, be subtle, and you can use espionage anywhere."
>
> *– Sun Tzu*

Banish all your thoughts of cloak-and-dagger mysteries, James Bond look-alikes or the misconception that only the morally ambiguous persons resort to using spies. Some time or other we may also have to become spies, for example, when we pass on information to certain 'friendly' quarters. Learn then to cultivate 'friendly' sources who will not hesitate to pass on information to us. Nurture the relationship with these persons carefully. If need be, reward them well. Be very careful to protect these persons for how else can we earn the trust of those who are willing to confide in us. Learn to distinguish what is real and what is not. If we can follow these rules, we should never be in want of information.

Applying The Art Of War

Memorandum 56

To : All Managers
From : General Manager's Office

Let us read Sun Tzu's essay, 'Espionage' further, which he closes the chapter and ends the book by saying:

"It is important to find out who are those sent by the enemy to spy on you, and bribe them to serve you instead. Tempt them with bribes and house them well. This way you not only convert them for your use but also get to recruit other agents living in the enemy's land or working for the enemy...Hence only the enlightened ruler and the wise general who are capable of using intelligent people as agents, can achieve great things. Secret operations are vital in war because on them depends the army's ability to make its move."

– Sun Tzu

It is not really surprising that some businessmen may try to place their own 'spies' in a rival's company. Two can always play the same game if the rival knows how to spot such spies and turn them around with kindness, money and other benefits. Therefore, we should always be on the alert for such tactics from our competitors.

We have finally come to the end of my interpretations of Sun Tzu's *Art of War*. In a month's time, I shall be leaving for my studies. I hope you have enjoyed reading and benefitted in some ways from Sun Tzu's philosophy as it applies to our work in the modern day. It is easy for me to write, easy for you to read, but most difficult for everyone of us to diligently apply Sun Tzu's words. But try.

Thank you and good luck.

PART II

ART OF WAR
The Full Text

chapter 1
PLANNING

Sun Tzu said:

The art of war is of vital importance to the state; the way of life or death; the road to safety or ruin. It is essential that it is studied seriously. Therefore, appraise it in terms of the five fundamental factors and compare the seven elements later named so that you may assess its importance.

The first of these factors is the moral law; the second, heaven; the third, earth; the fourth, command; and the fifth, doctrine.

By moral law, I mean that which causes the people to be in total accord with their ruler, so that they will follow him in life and unto death without fear for their lives and undaunted by any peril.

By heaven, I mean the working of natural forces; the effects of winter's cold and summer's heat and the conduct of military operations according to the seasons.

By earth, I mean whether the distances are great or short, whether the ground is easy or difficult to travel on, whether it is open ground or narrow passes, and the chances of life or death.

By command, I mean the general's stand for the virtues of wisdom, sincerity, benevolence, courage and strictness.

By doctrine, I mean the way the army is organised in its proper sub-divisions, the gradations of ranks among the officers, the maintenance of supply routes and the control of provisioning for the army.

There is no general who is unfamiliar with these five matters. Those who master them will win; those who do not will fail.

Therefore, when laying your plans, compare the following elements and appraise them carefully: Which ruler possesses the moral law; whose commander is the most capable; which army obtains the advantages of heaven and the earth; on which side are regulations and instructions carried out better; which army is the stronger; which has the better trained officers and men; and in which army is there certainty of rewards and punishments being dispensed with; I will be able to forecast which side will be victorious and which defeated.

A general who accepts my advice should be employed for he is certain to gain victory. A general who rejects my advice will meet defeat, and should be dismissed.

Once my beneficial advice is understood and followed, it will lay the foundation for the knowledge of war. Whenever any extraordinary problem arises, the knowledge gained will help to solve it. But this solid foundation should allow flexibility for one's advantage.

All warfare is based on deception. Therefore, when capable, pretend to be incapable; when active, inactive; when near, make the enemy believe that you are far away; when far away, that you are near. Hold out baits to lure the enemy; feign disorder and strike him. When he has the advantageous position, prepare against him; when he is strong, avoid him. If he is prone to choleric temper, irritate him. Pretend weakness so that he may become arrogant. If he is at ease, put him under a strain to wear him down. When his forces are united, divide them. Attack where he is unprepared; appear where you are least expected.

These are tactics used by a military strategist for victory and cannot be taught in advance.

One who foresees victory before battle, will mostly win. One who predicts not much of a chance of winning before the fight, will scarcely win.

More planning shall give more chances of victories while less planning, less chances of victory. So how about those without planning? By this measure, I can clearly foresee victory or defeat.

chapter 2
WAGING WAR

Sun Tzu said:

Operations of war shall normally require a thousand swift chariots, a thousand leather-covered wagons for carrying stores and a hundred thousand armoured troops, with food supplies transported over a thousand *li* (one *li* is approximately 0.35 mile).

Thus, the expenditure at home and along the way, for fees of advisers and visitors, materials for repair and maintenance, chariots and armour, can sum up to a thousand pieces of gold a day. Only then can an army of a hundred thousand soldiers be raised.

Victory is the main object in war. If this is long delayed, weapons are blunted and the ardour of the soldiers will be dampened.

When troops attack cities, their strength will be exhausted, and if the campaign is protracted, the resources of the state will not be enough to last the strain. When your weapons are dulled, your ardour dampened, your strength exhausted and treasure spent, other rulers will take advantage of your extremity to act. And then no man, however wise, will be able to avert the inevitable that follows.

Thus, while we have heard of stupid haste in war, we have not yet seen a clever operation that was prolonged. History has shown that there has never been a country benefitting from prolonged warfare.

Therefore, one who does not thoroughly understand the calamity of war shall not be able to thoroughly comprehend the advantage of the war.

The skilful general neither requires a second levy of conscripts nor more than one provision. They carry war materials from the homeland, but forage on the enemy. Thus, the army is plentifully provided with food.

When the treasury is impoverished, it is because military operations are being maintained from a distance; carriage of supplies for great distances renders the people destitute.

In the vicinity of the battle, things shall be extremely expensive. When the cost of living rises, people shall sink into poverty and then the government has to use force to exact taxes, thus exhausting the State's strength and finance.

The big battlefield shall become an empty shell with the peasantry losing seven-tenths of their property, while the Government shall incur expenditures for broken chariots, wornout horses, armours, arrows, crossbows, shields and supply wagons, amounting to six-tenths of its total revenue.

Hence the wise general sees to it that his troops feed on the enemy, for one cartload of the enemy's provisions is equivalent to twenty of his; one picul of enemy fodder to twenty from one's own store.

To kill the enemy is only out of impulsive rage; but to profit from his defeat is to gain over his wealth.

In battle, those who capture more than ten chariots from the enemy must be rewarded. Change the enemy's flags with our own, mix the captured chariots with ours for our use.

Be kind towards captives, and care for them. This is called "using the captured foe to strengthen one's own force."

In war, what matters is victory, not prolonged campaigns. And therefore the general who understands war is the arbiter of the people's fate and on him depends whether the nation shall be at peace or in danger.

chapter 3
OFFENSIVE STRATEGY

Sun Tzu said:

Generally, in war the best policy is to take the enemy's country whole and intact; to ruin it is not so good. Also, it is better to capture the enemy's army than to destroy it; to take intact a regiment, a company or a five-man squad is better than to destroy them.

Fighting to win one hundred victories in one hundred battles is not the supreme skill. To break the enemy's resistance without fighting is the supreme skill.

Thus, the general skilled in war places priority in attacking the enemy's strategy; the next best is to disrupt any alliances of the enemy; to be followed by the confrontation of his army.

The worst policy of all is to attack walled cities. Attack cities only as the last resort. The preparation of covered wagons, chariots and equipment requires three months; to pile up mounds against the walls shall take another three months.

If the general cannot control his anger and sends his soldiers to swarm up the walls like ants, then one-third of the troops will be killed without taking the city. Such is the calamity of the attack.

The skilful general subdues the enemy's army without fighting. He captures cities without laying siege and overthrows the enemy's reign without protracted operations. Aim to take All-Under-Heaven intact.

Thus, your troops are not wornout and your gains will be complete. This offensive strategy is that of using the sheathed sword.

The way of fighting is: if our force is ten times the enemy's, then surround him; five times his, attack him; if double his strength, divide our force into two to use as 'alternate strategy'; if only equal to his, we must concentrate our force to fight him.

When our casualties increase, withdraw. If our force is so much weaker than the enemy's, we should totally avoid him; if a small army is stubborn, it will only end up being captured by the larger enemy force.

A general is like the spoke of a wheel. If the connection is tied and complete, the wheel will be strong and so will be the State; if the connection is defective, then the State will be weak.

There are three ways whereby a ruler can bring misfortune upon his army: By commanding an army to advance or retreat, when ignorant on whether to advance or retreat. This is called 'hobbling the army.'

By trying to administer an army the same way he administers a kingdom, when ignorant of military affairs. This causes the officers to be perplexed.

By using the army officers without discrimination, when ignorant of the military principle of being flexible with circumstances. This causes doubts in the minds of the officers. When the army is confused and suspicious, neighbouring rulers will surely cause trouble.

Thus, there are five circumstances in which victory may be predicted: He who knows when he can fight and when not to fight will be victorious. He who understands the use of both large and small forces will win. He whose ranks are united in purpose will be victorious. He who is prepared and lies in wait for an enemy who is not, will be victorious. He who has capable generals and without interference by the ruler will be victorious. It is in these five matters that the way to victory is known.

Therefore, I say: If you know yourself and know your enemy; in a hundred battles you will never fear the result. When you know yourself but not your enemy, your chances of winning or losing are equal. If you know neither yourself nor your enemy, you are certain to be in danger in every battle.

chapter 4
TACTICS

Sun Tzu said:

Skilful warriors of ancient times first sought for themselves an invincible position whereby they will await the opportunity to strike at their enemy's vulnerability. Invincibility lies in one's own hands but the enemy's vulnerability is of his own making. Thus, those skilled in war can make themselves invincible but the enemy's vulnerability is provided only by the enemy himself.

Therefore, one may know how to win and yet is unable to do it. To be invincible, use defensive tactics; to make the enemy vulnerable, go on the offensive. Defend when one's strength is insufficient; attack when abundant.

Those skilled in defence appear to hide in the deepest nine-fold of the earth; those skilled in attack appear to move above the highest nine-fold of heaven. In this way, they can protect themselves and secure total victory.

To foresee a victory which others can also foresee is no great feat. There is no greatness in winning battles and being proclaimed universally as an expert, for to lift a rabbit's hair requires no great strength; to see the sun and moon is no sign of sharp sight; to hear the thunderclap is no sign of sharp hearing.

Tactics

What the ancients called a skilful fighter is one who not only wins but wins with ease. But the victories shall neither earn him reputation for wisdom nor credit for valour. For victories are such, they are gained in circumstances that have not been revealed and he thus wins no reputation for wisdom; and as the enemy submits without bloodshed, he receives no credit for valour.

He wins by making no mistakes. Making no mistakes means already having established the certainty of victory; conquering an enemy who is already defeated.

Therefore, a skilful commander puts himself in a position secured against defeat and misses no opportunity to defeat his enemy. In this way, the victorious army seeks battle only after the victory has been secured; an army destined to defeat fights in the hope of winning.

The good commander seeks virtues and goes about disciplining himself according to the laws so as to effect control over his success.

There are five methods in the military art: first, measurement; second, calculation; third, quantification; fourth, comparison; fifth, the possibility of winning.

Earth leads to measurement; measurement leads to calculation; calculation leads to quantification; quantification leads to comparison; comparison leads to the possibility of winning.

The victorious army is as twenty-four taels against one-twentieth of a tael; while the defeated army is one-twentieth of a tael against twenty-four taels.

The onrushing of the victorious soldiers, like the pent-up waters of a huge dam suddenly released to plunge down a thousand feet valley, is power!

chapter 5
ENERGY

Sun Tzu said:

Management of many is the same as management of a few. It is a matter of dividing up their numbers and functions.

Manoeuvering a large army is no different from manoeuvering a small one: it is a matter of formations and signals. In making sure the army can sustain the enemy's attack without suffering defeat, use direct and indirect manoeuvres.

Generally, in battle, use the direct methods to engage the enemy forces; indirect methods however are needed to secure victory.

In battle, there are only the direct or indirect methods of fighting but they give an endless combination of manoeuvres. For both forces are interlocked and using each will lead to the other; it is like moving in a circle – you can never come to an end. Who can determine where one ends and the other begins?

Torrential water tosses stones along in its course due to its momentum. The well-timed swoop of a hawk enables it to strike its prey. Therefore, the momentum of one who is skilled in war will be overwhelming and his decision to strike must be well-timed.

Energy is like a fully-drawn crossbow; the decision to strike is the timely release of the trigger.

Amid the turmoil and uproar of battle, the situation may appear to be chaotic and yet no real chaos exists; troops seem to be in disarray and yet cannot be routed. What is seen as confusion is actually good order; appearance of fear is in reality courage; appearance of weakness is yet true strength.

Order or disorder depends on organisation; concealing valour for a cowardly front is on circumstances; masking strength with weakness is to be effected by tactical disposition.

Thus, the skilful general keeps the enemy on the move by maintaining deceitful appearances; he holds out something that the enemy is certain to grab at, and with such baits keep the enemy going to where he lies in wait to strike.

A skilled commander conserves energy from the situation instead of wasting his men. He selects his men according to their talents and uses them to exploit the situation.

Hence, when he uses his men to fight, it is easy as moving logs and rocks. For the nature of logs and rocks, static when the ground is stable; mobile when the ground is uneven. Immobile if in the square-shape, rolling when round.

Thus, the energy generated in troops by a good commander, like the momentum of rolling a round boulder down a thousand feet mountain, is powerful!

chapter 6
WEAK AND STRONG POINTS

Sun Tzu said:

The one who is first to occupy the battlefield to await the enemy will be fresh and at ease; he who comes later to rush into the fight will be exhausted.

Therefore, the skilful commander imposes his will on the enemy by making the enemy come to him instead of being brought to the enemy.

To do this, he offers the enemy some advantages; and similarly, he is able to prevent the enemy's coming by inflicting damage on the enemy. When the enemy is taking his ease, harass him; when well-supplied with food, attack his supply lines to starve him out; when he is at rest, force him to move. Appear at those places that he must hasten to defend; move swiftly to those places where you are not expected.

That you may march a thousand *li* without exhaustion is due to the country being free of enemy troops. You can be sure of taking what you attack if you attack those places which are undefended. To ensure the safety of your position, hold only those positions that cannot be attacked.

For a general who is skilled in the offensive, the enemy would not know what to defend; and for one who is skilful in the defensive, the enemy would not know what to attack.

Subtle and secretive, the skilled learns to be invisible and silent to control the enemy's fate. He whose advance cannot be resisted makes for the enemy's weak areas; if need to withdraw, he moves so swiftly that he cannot be overtaken.

When I wish to fight, my enemy who may be sheltered by high ramparts and deep moats, can be forced to come out into an engagement if I were to attack a position that he will be obliged to relieve.

When I wish to avoid a fight, I can prevent an engagement even though the battlelines had been drawn by diverting my enemy with something odd and unexpected thrown in his way.

By discovering my enemy's dispositions and at the same time concealing mine from him, I can concentrate my forces while he must divide his. Knowing his dispositions, I can use my total strength against a part of his.

If he is ignorant of mine, he will have to spread out his forces to defend every point. This will give me superiority in numbers. And if I were to use my superior strength to attack an inferior one, those I deal with will be in dire straits.

The enemy must not know where I intend to attack. For if he knows not, he must prepare for possible attack in many places; and in such preparation, his forces shall be so spread out that those I have to fight with at any given point will be few.

Thus, when he prepares to defend the front, the rear will be weak; when he prepares to defend the rear, the front will weaken; similarly, left to right

Weak And Strong Points

and right to left. If he prepares to defend everywhere, he will be weak everywhere.

One who has few must prepare for defence; one who has many shall make the enemy prepare for defence.

When we know the place and the date of the battle, then even for a thousand *li*, we can march forth to engage the enemy.

But if knowing not where or when the enemy will attack, then our front and rear troops, left and right wings cannot protect each other. How much more then if troops are distanced by a hundred *li*, or even short of a few *li*?

As I see it, even though the number of soldiers of Yue exceeds ours, can that help them to win a battle? Thus, I can create victory. Even if the enemy is numerous, I can prevent him from fighting. Find out his plans to know which of his strategies will be successful and which will not. Provoke to agitate him and so learn the pattern of his movements. Force him to show his disposition and thus ascertaining his strengths and weaknesses.

The supreme skill in commanding troops is in the shapeless command. Then, the prying of the subtlest spies cannot penetrate for the laying of plans against you.

The shapes I take shall lay plans for victory but such are beyond the comprehension of the masses. While all can see the external aspects, none can understand the way I scored my victory.

Thus, when I win a victory, I do not repeat the tactics but respond to circumstances in limitless ways.

Military tactics are similar to water, for just as flowing water runs away from high places and speeds downwards, so an army avoids the strong enemy and strikes at the weak one. As water shapes its flow according to the ground, an army wins by relating to the enemy it faces. And just as water retains no constant shape, in war there shall be no constant conditions.

Thus, the one who can modify his tactics according to the enemy's situations shall be victorious and may be called The Divine Commander.

For none of the five elements (water, fire, wood, metal and earth) is always predominant; none of the four seasons can last forever; and days sometimes are longer, sometimes shorter; the moon sometimes waxes or wanes.

chapter 7

MANOEUVRES

Sun Tzu said:

Without harmony in the State, no military expedition can be made; without harmony in the army, no battle formation can be directed. In war, the general first receives his commands from the ruler. He then assembles his troops and blends them into a harmonious entity before pitching camp.

Nothing is more difficult than directing manoeuvres. The difficulty lies in turning the devious into the direct, and misfortune into gain.

Thus, adopt an indirect route and divert the enemy by enticing him with a bait. Once done, you may march forth after he has gone and arrive before him. One who is able to do this knows the strategy of the direct and indirect.

But while manoeuvres can offer advantages, they also pose dangers.

When one sets in motion an entire army to chase an advantage, the chances are that he will not attain it.

If one abandons the camp to fight for an advantage, he will have to give up heavy equipment. Thus, in rolling up the armour to chase incessantly day and night, marching at double time for a hundred *li*, the commanders will only fall into enemy's hands. This is because the stronger soldiers will arrive first while the feeble ones will fall behind, and by this method, only one-tenth of the troops will arrive.

In a forced march of fifty *li*, the front commander will fall and only half the troops will arrive. In a forced march of thirty *li*, then two-thirds will arrive.

An army cannot survive without its equipment, food and stores.

If we cannot fathom the designs of our neighbouring States, we cannot enter into alliances in advance.

Those who do not know the conditions of mountains, forests, high and dangerous grounds, defiles, marshes and swamps, cannot conduct the march of an army.

Those who do not use local guides cannot benefit from the advantages of the ground.

War is based on deception. Move only if there is a real advantage to be gained and create changes in the situation by dividing or concentrating your forces.

Be swift as the wind, compact as the forest. In raiding and plundering, like fire; in stability, as the mountain. Let your plans be unfathomable as the clouds and move like the thunderbolt.

When plundering the countryside and having captured new lands, divide the profits among our men. Observe and assess the situation before making our move.

Winners are those who know the art of direct and indirect strategies. Such is the art of military manoeuvres.

The Book of Military Administration says: "As orders cannot be heard clearly in the battlefield, so make use of bells and drums. As soldiers cannot distinguish each other in the confusing battle situation, so use flags and banners."

For drums and bells, flags and banners are to unify the sight and hearing of a person. When soldiers are thus united, the brave cannot advance alone and the coward also cannot withdraw. This is the art of controlling a large army.

Use torches and drums in night fighting, and use flags and banners in day fighting, as a means of influencing the enemy's sight and hearing.

An army may be robbed of its spirit and the commander be robbed of his wits. In the morning a soldier's spirit is keenness, during the day, it gradually diminishes, and in the evening, the soldier thinks only of returning to camp.

Thus, the skilful commander avoids the enemy whose spirit is at its keenness and instead attacks only when the enemy's spirit is sluggish and thinking of camp. This is control of the spirit.

Prepare ourselves in good order to await a disorderly enemy; in calmness, await a boisterous one. This is control of the mind.

Close to the battlefield, wait for the enemy coming from afar: at ease, await a tired enemy; with well-fed troops, await hungry ones. This is control of strength.

Do not engage an enemy whose banners are in perfect order or whose troops are arrayed in an impressive formation. This is control of circumstances.

Therefore, in accordance with military axioms, do not advance against the enemy who occupies higher ground; do not oppose him if he comes downhill.

Do not pursue an enemy who pretends to flee. Refrain from attacking troops whose spirit is keen. Do not swallow baits put out by the enemy. Avoid stopping enemy troops on the home march. When surrounding an enemy, leave him an escape route. Do not press an enemy to desperation. This is the way of manoeuvering an army.

chapter 8

TACTICAL VARIATIONS

Sun Tzu said:

In war, a general first receives commands from the ruler, then gathers the people, and assembles the troops.

Never encamp on swampy grounds.

Keep the ground for communication opened so that you may contact your allies.

Do not linger on grounds which are dangerously isolated.

When trapped on grounds which are hemmed-in, use stratagem to break out.

In death ground where desperation demands, fight.

There are some roads which we must not follow; some enemy troops we must not fight; some cities we must not attack; some grounds we must not contest; even some orders from the ruler which we must not obey.

A general who thoroughly understands the use of the nine variations, knows how to command an army.

A general who does not understand the nine variations, although familiar with the ground, will still be unable to take advantage of this familiarity.

In military operations, one who lacks the knowledge of the nine tactical variations, even if he has knowledge of the 'five advantages,' will still be unable to use his troops effectively.

A wise general considers both the advantages and disadvantages opened to him. When considering the advantages, he makes his plan feasible; when considering the disadvantages, he finds ways to extricate himself from the difficulties.

Therefore, seek to reduce those hostile neighbouring States by bringing harm to them. Labour them with constant trifle affairs. Lead them by their noses with superficial offers of advantages.

It is a principle of war that we do not assume the enemy will not come, but instead we must be prepared for his coming; not to presume he will not attack, but instead to make our own position unassailable.

There are five dangerous faults which a general should not have in his character. Recklessness, which leads to destruction; cowardice, which ends in capture; a quick temper, which enables you to make him look foolish; delicacy in honour, which causes sensitivity to shame; overly compassionate for his men, which exposes him to worry and harassment. These five faults in a general can seriously ruin military operations.

chapter 9
ON THE MARCH

Sun Tzu said:

When positioning the army in order to observe the enemy, cross over the mountains and stay close to valleys. Position in high ground with a wide view.

Never ascend to attack but only fight downhill. This is mountain positioning.

After crossing a river, we must keep away from it. When the enemy crosses the river towards us, do not engage him in mid-stream. It will be advantageous to wait until half of the enemy troops are ashore, and then attack.

If we wish to fight, do not confront the enemy near the river. Choose a high position with a wide view. Never position downstream. This is river positioning.

Avoid swamps but if there is a need to cross them, do so quickly and without delay. If forced to fight in swamps, keep close to grass and have the trees to your rear. This is positioning in swamps.

In level ground, choose a position easy to move and easy to get your supply. With higher ground to the right and the rear, open plain in front and safety to the rear. This is positioning in level ground.

All these four methods of positioning armies were used by the Yellow Emperor when he conquered the four neighbouring countries.

An army prefers high ground to low; sunny places to cold wet shades. Nourish your soldiers and build up their internal strength so that they are free of hundreds of diseases, and this will ensure victory.

When near hills, mounds, embankments or dikes, take up the position that faces the sun and have higher ground to the right and rear. This is to benefit from the natural advantages of the ground.

When crossing a river with much bubbles in the water, this means there were heavy rains at the upper stream, and we should wait until the water subsides and calms down before crossing.

Whenever there are torrents, 'Heavenly Wells,' 'Heavenly Prisons,' 'Heavenly Nets,' 'Heavenly Traps,' and 'Heavenly Gaps,' get away quickly. Do not go near them.

I keep away from them and lure the enemy towards them. I face the enemy and force him to put his back to them.

When on the march, there are dangerous defiles, swamps with aquatic grass and reeds, forests with dense tangled undergrowth, which must be carefully and repeatedly searched out, for these are the places where the enemy can lay ambushes or hide spies.

When the enemy is near but remains quiet, this means he is confidently relying on his impregnable position.

When the enemy is far but keeps on challenging, he is trying to lure us to advance.

If the enemy takes up a position that is easy for us to discover and attack, he could be offering an ostensible advantage to trap us. When there is movement amongst the trees, we know the enemy is advancing.

When obstacles are set up in the undergrowth, the enemy is seeking to deceive us.

Birds that suddenly rise in flight shows that there are men hiding in ambush positions; wild animals scurrying shows the enemy is making surprise advances.

When dust rises in high columns, this shows chariots are rushing forward; when dust is low and widespread, infantry is approaching.

When dust is scattered in different directions, the enemy is gathering firewood; when dust clouds are few and moving to and fro, the enemy is encamping his army.

When the enemy's envoys speak humbly but he is secretly preparing his force, he will advance.

But when the language is fierce and the enemy threatens to attack, he is looking for a way to retreat.

When his chariots take up positions at both wings, he is ready to fight.

When without a previous understanding, the enemy presents peace proposals, he must be plotting.

When enemy troops are seen running about and getting into formations, then the 'expectant date' of attack as forewarned by the enemy's spies is drawing near.

When half his force is advancing and half is withdrawing, he is putting out a bait.

When his soldiers lean on their weapons, they are weakened by hunger.

When those sent to draw water rush to drink before carrying back to camp, the troops are suffering from water shortage.

When the enemy sees an advantage but makes no effort to advance and seize it, his army is exhausted.

When birds gather around the camp, it has been vacated.

When soldiers shouts loudly at night, they are nervous.

When the troops are in disorder, the general has lost his authority. When the flags and banners are shifted about, the army is in chaos. If the officers are short-tempered, they are tired.

When the troops feed grain to their horses, slaughter the transport cattle for food, and do not hang up their cooking pots properly or do not return to their shelters, they are desperate and are preparing to fight to the death.

When troops are seen whispering amongst themselves in small groups, the general has lost the confidence of his men.

Too frequent rewards show the general is losing control over his men as only rewards can keep them in even temper. Too frequent punishments show him to be in dire distress as nothing else can keep them in check.

If the officers at first treat their men harshly and later fear them, the limit of indiscipline is reached. When the enemy sends envoys to apologise, this shows he wants a truce.

When facing enemy troops who are in high spirits for some time without either joining battle or withdrawing, we must carefully analyse and observe the situation.

In battle, having more soldiers will not necessarily secure victory. Never advance by relying blindly on the strength of military power. It is sufficient to concentrate our strength, estimate the enemy's position and seek his capture. But anyone who lacks consideration and treats the enemy with contempt and disdain will only end up being captured.

Secure the loyalty of your troops first before punishing them or they will not be submissive. When they are loyal and if punishment is not enforced, you still cannot use them.

Therefore, treat your men kindly but keep strict control over them to ensure victory. If the commands used in training troops are consistent, soldiers will be disciplined. If not, soldiers are inclined to be disobedient. If a general's commands are consistently credible and obeyed, he enjoys good relationship between him and his men.

chapter 10
TERRAIN

Sun Tzu said:

There are six types of ground befitting its nature: open, entangling, inconclusive, narrow, precipitous and distant.

Open ground is that which can be easily traversed by both sides. In such ground, we must occupy the higher position which faces the sun and is convenient for our supply routes so that we can fight with advantage.

It is easy to enter into entangling ground but difficult to withdraw from. In such ground, if the enemy is unprepared, our attack will certainly dislodge them. But if he is prepared and our attack fails to defeat him, then it would be difficult to retreat. This is the disadvantage of this ground.

Ground which is disadvantageous for both the enemy and ourselves is inconclusive ground. In such ground, do not advance to take the enemy's baits but instead seek to lure him forward by our retreat. Wait until half of his force has advanced, then attack to gain an advantage.

We must occupy narrow ground first, then block up the passes and await the enemy. If the enemy has already occupied it, follow him only if he has yet to block up the passes; if he has done so, then do not follow.

On precipitous ground, we must occupy the higher ground which faces the sun first and await the enemy. If the enemy has already occupied it, lure him to leave but never follow him in.

If we are at a distance from an enemy of equal strength, then it is difficult to engage him successfully.

These six grounds are the principles of Earth. It is the highest responsibility of a general to observe and study them.

When troops are inclined to flee, insubordinate against commands, distressed, disorganised, or defeated, it is the fault of the general as none of these calamities arises from natural causes.

When other conditions are equal, if an army is outnumbered by ten to one, then the soldiers of the weaker force are certain to flee.

When the common soldiers are stronger than their officers, they will insubordinate.

When the officers are too strong and the troops are weak, the result is collapse.

When senior officers are angry and go against orders, and they fight on meeting the enemy without being told by their general whether such is feasible or not, the result is defeat.

When the general is morally weak and lacks authority; when his instructions are not clear; when there are no consistent rules to guide both officers and men, and the ranks are slovenly formed, the result is disorganisation.

When a general fails to size up his enemy and uses an inferior force to engage a larger one, or weak troops to attack the strong, or neglects to place picked men in the front ranks, the result is a rout.

These six conditions shall lead to failure. It is also the highest responsibility of a general to study them carefully.

Conformation of the terrain is the soldier's best ally in battle. Thus, victory rests with the superior general who can size up his enemy and provide for the distances in travel and the nature of the land with all its difficulties. He who understands this theory and uses it to conduct the fight will certainly win; he who does not will fail.

If the situation offers victory but the ruler forbids fighting, the general may still fight. If the situation is such that he cannot win, then the general must not fight even if the ruler orders him to do so.

Thus, the general who advances without coveting fame and withdraws without fearing disgrace, but whose sole intention is to protect the people and do good service for his ruler, is the precious jewel of the State.

Such a general who protects his soldiers like infants will have them following him into the deepest valleys. A general who treats his soldiers like his own beloved sons will have their willingness to die with him.

But if he is too indulgent; if he loves them too much to enforce his commands; and cannot assert control when the troops are in disorder: Then the soldiers are similar to spoilt children and shall became useless.

If I know my soldiers are capable of attacking the enemy but am unaware that he is invulnerable to attack, my chance of victory is but half.

If I know the enemy is open to attack but do not know my soldiers are incapable of attacking him, my chance of victory is but half.

If I know the enemy can be attacked and my soldiers are capable of doing it but am unaware that the terrain is unsuited for fighting, I should hold back for my chance of victory is but half.

Thus, when those skilled in war make their move, there is no mistake; when they act, they have unlimited resources. So I say: know your enemy, know yourself and your victory will be undoubted. Know Earth and know Heaven and your victory will be complete.

chapter 11

THE NINE VARIETIES OF GROUND

Sun Tzu said:

In commanding an army, classify ground into nine varieties: dispersive, frontier, key, open, intersecting, vital, difficult, enclosed and death.

When a feudal lord fights in his own territory, he is in dispersive ground.

When he penetrates slightly into the territory of others, he is in frontier ground. Ground that gives advantage to any warring party is a key ground.

Ground that is accessible by both the warring parties is open ground.

The ground that is enclosed by three States and whoever is first in occupying it will gain the support of All-Under-Heaven is intersecting ground.

When the army has advanced deep into the enemy's territory, leaving many enemy cities and towns behind, it is vital ground.

When the army marches through mountains, forests, precipitous land, swamps, or any place that is dangerous to march, it is in difficult ground.

Ground that has a narrow access and tortuous exit, whereby the smaller enemy force can crush my larger one, is enclosed ground.

Ground in which only a desperate fight may offer survival is death ground.

The Nine Varieties Of Ground

Therefore, do not fight in dispersive ground; do not halt in frontier ground; do not attack an enemy who has already occupied key ground; do not break up our formations into separate units in open ground.

Ally with neighbouring States in intersecting ground; plunder in vital ground.

In difficult ground, keep on moving; in enclosed ground, use strategies; in death ground, fight.

Those skilful commanders of old knew how to split the enemy's unity between the front and rear troops; to prevent cooperation between the main force and the reinforcement; to hinder the stronger troops from rescuing the weaker ones, and subordinates from supporting their superiors.

Disperse the enemy troops and prevent them from assembling; even though his soldiers are gathered, they will be in disorder.

We move when there is advantage to gain; we halt when there is none.

Should one ask: "If attacked by a large and orderly enemy troops, what shall I do?" I would reply: "Seize something that he holds dear so that he has no choice but to yield to your will."

Speed is the essence of war. Take advantage of the enemy's lack of preparation; move by using unexpected routes and attack where he has made no defence.

When we are deep in the enemy's territory, be 'the guest of our enemy'; the deeper we penetrate, the more united will be our soldiers and the enemy cannot overcome us.

Plunder the fertile countryside to get enough food for our army.

Give attention to the well-being of your men; do not unnecessarily exhaust them. Keep their spirit united; conserve their energy.

Do not let your enemy understand the plans concerning your troops' movements. Put your men in positions where there is no escape and even when facing death, they will not run. In preparing for death, what is there that cannot be achieved? Both officers and men will do their best. In a desperate situation, they lose their sense of fear; without a way out, they shall stand firm. When they are deep within enemy territory they are bound together and without an alternative, they will fight hard.

Thus, without need of supervision, they will be alert, and without being asked, they will support their general; without being ordered, they will trust their general. If my officers are not exceedingly rich, it is not that they disdain wealth. If they do not expect long life, it is not due to dislike for longevity.

On the day the army is ordered to march, soldiers who are seated will cry till their lapels are soaked; the tears of those who are reclining will wet their cheeks. But once they are thrown into battle where there is no escape, they will show incredible courage like that of Chuan Chu and Ts'ao Kuei.

Thus, a good general commands the army like the *shuai-ran*, a huge snake found in the Ch'ang mountains. When struck on the head, its tail attacks; when struck on the tail, its head attacks; when struck in the middle, both head and tail attack.

Should someone ask: "Can an army be commanded like the *shuai-ran*?", I would answer: "Yes." The people of Wu and Yue mutually hate each other but when they sail in the same boat tossed by the wind, they will help each other just like the right hand cooperates with the left.

Therefore, the burying of wheels deep into the soil to stabilise the chariot or the tethering of the war horses is not sufficient to place one's dependance upon.

In military administration, cultivate a uniform level of courage. Make use of the advantage of the ground so as to bring out the best of both strong and weak soldiers. A wise general thus leads the entire army like he is leading one person.

It is the business of a general to be calm and mysterious; fair and composed. He must be capable of mystifying his officers and men so that they are ignorant of his true intentions.

He forbids the casting of omens and do away with superstitious beliefs that even until the time of death, no calamity need be feared.

He changes his arrangements and alters his plans so that no one knows what he is up to. He changes campsites and takes circuitous routes to prevent others from anticipating his purpose.

He leads the army into battle just like a person who has climbed to the heights and then kicks away the ladder behind him so as to put them into a desperate position.

His business is to assemble his troops and throw them into a critical position. He leads them deep into enemy's territory to further his plans.

He burns the boats and breaks the cooking pots; like one shepherding a flock of sheep, he drives the army here, there, and none knows where he is going.

The changes of the nine varieties of ground gives varying advantages of attacking and defending; and the behaviour of the soldiers are matters which must be studied seriously.

When our army advances into enemy's territory, be his guest and if our penetration is deep and our soldiers know there is no turning back, they will concentrate their fighting spirit; if our penetration is shallow and soldiers are still thinking of home, their spirit will be distracted.

After leaving our own country, march our army across the border and we are in frontier ground. When there are convergence of all roads from different directions, that is open ground.

When we have penetrated deeply into the enemy's territory, that is vital ground. Shallow penetration is frontier ground. When the enemy's force is solidly to our rear and we face a narrow pass in front, we are in enclosed ground. A place with no way to turn to is death ground. Therefore, when in dispersive ground, I will unify soldiers'

The Nine Varieties Of Ground

fighting spirit; in frontier ground, I will make sure that our troops are well linked up. In key ground, I will rush up our rear troops; in open ground, I will increase our vigilance; in intersecting ground, I will strengthen my alliance; in vital ground, I will make sure continued provisions are safeguarded; in difficult ground, I will push the army to march on; in enclosed ground, I will block the passes; in death ground, I will show the soldiers that there is no way to survive but to fight.

For the nature of soldiers is such: when surrounded, will defend; when desperate, will fight; when in peril, will obey promptly.

If we cannot fathom the designs of our neighbouring States, we cannot enter into alliances in advance. Those who do not know the conditions of mountains, forests, high and dangerous grounds, defiles, marshes and swamps, cannot conduct the march of an army. Those who do not use local guides cannot benefit from the advantages of the ground.

To be ignorant of the nine varieties of the ground is not befitting the command of the army of the Supreme King.

When the army of the Supreme King attacks a large State, the latter shall be unable to concentrate its force. Being thus intimidated by its might, the allies of the large State will not dare come to its aid.

There is neither the need to fight the combined States nor is there any need to foster the power of the other States. The Supreme King's army can rely on its own ability to overawe its enemies. It can thus conquer their cities and destroy their kingdoms.

Bestow rewards without regard to customary rules, issue orders without regard to prescribed procedures. Thus, you may run the entire army as you would one man.

Assign tasks to your soldiers without detailing your plan. Show them the advantages without revealing the dangers. Put them into a perilous spot and they will survive; trap them on death ground and they will fight for their lives. For only when the army is in danger that they can turn defeat into victory.

To be successful in warfare, we must pretend we are keeping to the enemy's designs. Concentrate your forces against him and then you can kill his general from a thousand *li* away. This is called achieving your task in a tricky and artful way.

On the day of commencing the attack, seal off the passes, cancel all passports, have no more contact with the enemy's envoys, seriously speak in the temple on the decision for the battle.

Whenever the enemy presents an opportunity, take it quickly. Anticipate him by seizing what he holds dear, check the situation of his force, and secretly fix a day to launch the attack.

Therefore, at the start of the battle, be as coy as a virgin; when the enemy lowers his guard and offers an opening, rush in like a hare out of its cage and the enemy will be unable to defend in time.

chapter 12
ATTACK BY FIRE

Sun Tzu said:

There are five methods of attacking with fire: first, to burn soldiers in their camp or towns; second, to burn stores; third, to burn transportation; fourth, to burn arsenals; and the fifth, to fire torched arrows into enemy's camp to create chaos and disorder.

There must be a good reason for using fire and the equipment must be prepared and available.

The weather and timing must be right for attacking with fire. Dry weather is essential. The timing should be when the moon is at the following positions: 'star of the green dragon' (eastern); 'star of martial enigma' (northern); 'star of the white tiger' (western); and 'star of the red sparrow' (southern). For these are the days of rising wind.

To attack by fire, we should respond differently according to the five methods of attack.

If fire is started in the enemy's camp by our undercover spies, we should respond by attacking immediately. When fire breaks out but his soldiers remain calm, then we must wait instead of rushing in to attack for there must be some ruse afoot.

When the fire burns to an uncontrollable inferno, follow up with an attack if the situation allows; otherwise, wait.

The right weather and timing can allow you to trigger off the fire attack from without instead of from within. Set fire according to the direction of the wind, not against it.

Generally, when it is windy the whole day, the night will be calm; observe this accurately.

All armies must possess knowledge of these five different methods of attacking with fire, keep vigilance of the weather and the enemy's condition.

Thus, to attack by fire is intelligent for the effect is fast and obvious.

Attack by water only on the condition we have a very strong army, for water can result in isolating the enemy's troops but cannot destroy his supplies or equipment, thus not so effective.

Therefore, to win battles and make conquests and to take over all the subjects but failing to rebuild or restore the welfare of what he gains would be a bad omen, so called 'wasteful stay'.

The enlightened ruler plans well ahead, and good generals serve to execute the plans.

Do not act unless it is in the interest of the State. Do not use your troops unless you can win. Do not fight unless you are in danger.

No ruler should put troops into the field because he is angry; no general should fight because he is resentful. Move when there is benefit to be gained, quit when there is no more advantage. For an angry man can later become happy, a resentful man become pleased, but a kingdom once destroyed can never be restored nor the dead be brought back to life.

Hence the enlightened ruler is prudent and the good general should not be hasty. Thus a country is safe and the army preserved.

chapter 13
'A CRACK BETWEEN TWO DOORS' (ESPIONAGE)

Sun Tzu said:

To raise an army of a hundred thousand soldiers and march them a thousand *li* to battle entails heavy burden on both the people and the State's treasury, as expenses can amount to a thousand pieces of gold a day. There will be chaos at home and abroad, and soldiers and people shall both be exhausted on the routes causing the affairs of seven hundred thousand households to be abandoned.

He who faces an enemy for many years, to struggle for the victory that can be decided in a single day and yet remains ignorant of the enemy's position because he begrudges giving ranks, honours and a few hundred pieces of gold, is totally without humanity. Such a man is no leader, no help to his ruler, no master of victory.

The enlightened ruler and the wise general can subdue the enemy whenever they move and they can achieve superhuman feats because they have foreknowledge. This foreknowledge cannot be obtained from spirits, gods, or by reasoning over past events, or by calculations. It can only be obtained from men who know the enemy position.

There are five classes of spies: native, inside, converted, condemned and surviving.

'A Crack Between Two Doors' (Espionage)

When these five classes of spies are all at work simultaneously and none can penetrate their operations, they are called the "spiritual and mystic web of threads" and are the treasures of a ruler.

Native spies are those living in the enemy's country whom we employ as suppliers of reliable information.

Inside spies are those dissatisfied enemy officials whom we bribe for valuable information.

Converted spies are really the enemy's spies whom we feed with false information or make use of to spread rumours so as to lure the enemy into our traps.

Condemned spies are our spies who shall pretend to turn traitors so as to supply false information to the enemy or our spies who have been deliberately fed with false information and then shall suffer capture by the enemy. They will certainly be executed when the enemy realises the deceit.

Surviving spies are our spies who are selected for extremely tough and high-intelligence undercover missions within the enemy's territory. They are expected to make use of all means to learn and collect information before sneaking back to report.

The relationship between the commander and his secret agent is more intimate than all others in the army. The rewards given to secret agents are more liberal than any other given.

The confidentiality given to secret operations is greater than for other matters. Only the one who is wise and sagely, benevolent and just, can use secret agents. Only he who is sensitive and subtle can get the truth of their reports.

Be subtle, be subtle, and you can use espionage anywhere.

Subtle, and most delicate, there is no means that cannot be used in espionage.

If the secret mission leaks out before an operation, then the spy and those whom he has spoken to should all be put to death.

Whichever army you wish to attack, city you wish to conquer, or person whom you wish to assassinate, you must know the names of the commanders, chief assistants, bodyguards, sentries and other subordinates, so make your spies check and acquire these facts accurately.

It is important to find out who are those sent by the enemy to spy on you and bribe them to serve you instead. Tempt them with bribes and house them well. This way you not only convert them for your use but also get to recruit other agents living in the enemy's land or working for the enemy. It is also in this manner that condemned spies, fed with false informations can be sent to cheat enemy. By this way too surviving spies can be sent to accomplish their tasks and return in due time. As a ruler, have total understanding about the activities of the five classes of spies. This knowledge comes mostly from converted spies and they must be treated with great importance. In ancient times, when Yin succeeded Hsia in power, it was due to I-Chih who as Chief Minister of Hsia was responsible for the State's affairs; then, when Chou succeeded Yin, it was Lu Ya, the former Minister of

Yin, who helped Chou to construct the solid foundation for a glorious dynasty of twenty-nine generations. Hence only the enlightened ruler and the wise general who are capable of using intelligent people as agents, can achieve great things. Secret operations are vital in war because the army's ability to make its move depends on them.

PART III
Application by Famous Characters

Some Famous Characters In
Ancient Chinese Military History Who
Applied Or Neglected To Apply The
ART OF WAR

OF CRAFTY COMMANDERS WHO KNEW HOW TO USE DECEIT IN WAR

A. **Sun Pin (a descendant of Sun Tzu)**
In 341BC, the States of Wei and Zhao combined to attack Han whose ruler appealed to the King of Qi for help. The task of relieving Han fell on Qi's commander-in-chief, T'ien Chi.

On the advice of Sun Pin, his chief of staff, T'ien Chi marched directly for Ta Liang, the capital of Wei, thus forcing Wei's commander-in-chief, Pang Chuan, to break off his assault on Han in order to return to his own country's defence.

Sun Pin, wishing to take advantage of Wei's contempt for the bravery of the Qi troops, advised T'ien Chi to have a hundred thousand cooking fires built on the first night of entering the land of Wei, fifty thousand on the following night, and further reduced to thirty thousand on the third night.

When this advice was followed, and the sightings were accordingly reported to Pang Chuan, he was greatly pleased, saying: "I have always known the men of Qi were cowards. They have been in Wei for only three days and more than half their numbers have already deserted."

Bolstered by his confidence, he left his heavily armoured infantry and chariots behind, taking only lightly-armed troops to pursue and confront the Qi forces.

The Wei troops, thus deceived, were subsequently routed and Pang Chuan committed suicide.

B. Chuko Liang

During the Three Kingdoms Period (AD220 to AD280), Chuko Liang, the Prime Minister and commander-in-chief of Shu was camped at Yang P'ing when he was forced to send the bulk of his troops to relieve Shu's eastern territory.

He was thus left with few troops and his enemy, Ssuma-I, Wei's commander-in-chief, upon hearing the news from his spies, immediately rushed troops to Yang P'ing to capture Chuko Liang.

When the Wei troops were sighted, Chuko Liang did not panic but instead ordered his men to unfurl their banners and flags, silence their war-drums, open the four gates of the city and keep out of sight.

While a few men were seen sweeping the streets and sprinkling water to keep down the dust, Chuko Liang appeared in a gate tower where he calmly sat to play his lute.

At this unexpected sight, Ssuma-I immediately suspected an ambush and withdrew his troops in great haste. It was thus that Chuko Liang later made good his escape and rejoined his main army where he told his chief of staff: "I knew Ssuma-I has a suspicious nature and thus thinking I had prepared an ambush for him, he led away his men when they could have easily captured me."

Needless to say, when Ssuma-I later learned how he was fooled by Chuko Liang, he was most upset.

OF CAPABLE COMMANDERS WHO KNEW HOW TO HANDLE TROOPS

A. Wu Ch'i

Wu Ch'i (430BC to 381BC), a general who lived during the Warring States Period, was known to wear the same clothes and eat the same food as the lowliest of his soldiers. He would rather sleep on rough ground than on a mattress, and when on the march, he would not mount his horse but would get in step with his men and carry his own rations.

He was however a strict disciplinarian. When he was fighting the Xin forces, one of his officers rode out of his ranks without permission to engage the enemy in individual combats. Although that officer succeeded in killing two of the enemy's men, Wu Ch'i ordered him to be executed. When the army commissioner spoke up for the condemned man's bravery, Wu Ch'i said: "I know he is brave but he is disobedient."

Even though he was strict with his men, the fact that he shared the exhaustion and bitter toil with his troops won him their respect and affection.

When the mother of one of his soldiers heard that Wu Ch'i personally sucked out the poison from her son's sore, she began wailing and lamenting. She was reproached by a friend who said: "Why do you cry? You ought to be proud for your son is only a common soldier and yet his commander-in-chief has done this unpleasant task for him."

The woman replied: "When Lord Wu did the same for my husband many years ago, my husband thereafter never left his side and finally died in battle for the lord. Now this has happened to my son, he too will die fighting though I know not when."

B. Ts'ao Ts'ao

Ts'ao Ts'ao (AD155 to AD220) who was made King of Wei by the Han Emperor Hsien Ti in AD216 was a skilful military strategist. When facing his enemies, he kept up the appearance of calmness and not given to fighting but the moment an opportunity presents itself, he would strike without hesitation.

A good judge of men, he personally picked them out from the rank-and-file and groomed them for important positions as generals, governors or prefects, thus strengthening his hold on his kingdom.

Although frugal by nature, he was however not one to consider a thousand pieces of gold too much when acknowledging and rewarding meritorious services.

He too was a strict disciplinarian. Once, when leading an expedition against rebels, he had to cross a wheat-field and wishing to gain the support of the peasants in the area, he ordered his troops to dismount and lead their horses across the field so as to prevent damage to the crops.

However, his horse was so startled by a screeching bird which suddenly flew out of some bushes that it trampled some of the crops. Ts'ao

Ts'ao immediately summoned the executioner and ordered his own execution.

When his generals and aides tearfully remonstrated that the army could not progress without its commander-in-chief, only then would he agree to stay his own execution. Instead he cut off a lock of his hair to show that even a commander-in-chief is not above the law.

The lock of hair was then displayed to the soldiers whom thereafter took great care to obey the laws set by their superiors.

OF WISE COMMANDERS WHO KNEW THE VALUE OF TOLERANCE

A. King Kou Chien

During the Spring and Autumn Period (722BC to 481BC), the State of Yue was subjugated into being a vassal of the State of Wu. King Kou Chien, together with other hostages, were forced to live in Wu to serve King Fu Chai.

For three years King Kou Chien tolerated his humiliation and served King Fu Chai without complaint. And to remind himself of his country's shame and his own bitterness, he slept on a bed of tree branches and tasted from time to time a bitter gall which he hung up by his bedside in the stables where he had his lodging.

When he was deemed as 'not dangerous' and allowed to return to Yue, King Kou Chien assisted by his loyal general, Fan Li, thereafter raised an army and succeeded in extinguishing Wu in 474BC and killing King Fu Chai to recover his own country.

B. Ssuma-I

Towards the latter part of the Three Kingdoms Period (AD220 to AD280), the Shu forces invaded the State of Wei.

Wei's commander-in-chief, Ssuma-I, took up positions to check the Shu troops but concentrated all his efforts towards fortification of his positions instead of engaging the Shu troops in decisive combat. To the chagrin and frustration of his of-

Application By Famous Characters

ficers, he also issued orders prohibiting them from engaging in individual combats with any of the enemy officers who came up daily to hurl challenges and insults at the defenders.

When Shu's commander-in-chief tried to goad Ssuma-I into combat by sending him a scornful gift of a woman's head-dress, all of the Wei's officers begged permission to rush into battle immediately to avenge the insult. They were rebuked by Ssuma-I who said: "If the slight cannot be tolerated, the big scheme will be upset."

After more waiting, Ssuma-I suddenly gave orders to attack the Shu troops whose dead piled up and the survivors were sent fleeing back to their own country.

Ssuma-I later explained that when the Shu troops first came to Wei, their fighting spirit was keen. But by postponing the fight, not only the enemy's food supplies were diminished, they had also begun to miss their homes and lost their ardour to fight.

OF DETERMINED COMMANDERS WHO KNEW HOW TO TURN A DISADVANTAGE INTO AN ADVANTAGE

A. T'ien Tan

In 279BC, the Yen army surrounded Chi Mo in the State of Qi. The Qi general, T'ien Tan openly expressed his fear of the Yen army cutting off the noses of their Qi prisoners and using these prisoners as human shields in the front of the fighting.

On being informed of this speech, the Yen commanders immediately ordered the act be done, and the Qi defenders were enraged to see their countrymen so mutilated and used. Fearing that they would suffer the same fate if they were to fall into the enemy's hands, they willed themselves to fight to the death.

T'ien Tan next arranged for his converted spies to report his other fear to the enemy: "I am in dread of the men of Yen exhuming the ancestral graves outside the city and inflicting indignity upon our ancestors." Again, the Yen troops set themselves to despoil the graves and burning the corpses in the sight of the defenders, causing the Qi citizens to burn with rage.

Knowing his men were ready to fight, T'ien Tan played his final cards – he replaced the regular soldiers manning the city's walls with the old and weaker men and women, and sent forth envoys bearing 24,000 ounces of silver to the Yen general, Ch'i Chieh, pleading on behalf of the wealthier citizens to spare their families and homes when the city surrenders.

The Yen army became increasingly relaxed and negligent in their arrogance, and were thus caught unprepared when T'ien Tan's soldiers drove forth a thousand painted-oxen with the rushes tied to their tails set on fire. In the savage attack, Ch'i Chieh perished and the Yen army fled in disorder.

Instead of losing Chi Mo to the enemy, this battle enabled T'ien Tan to recover some 70 cities which Qi previously lost to Yen.

B. Fu Yen-Ch'ing

In AD945 a vast host of Khitan (a nomadic tribe) warriors surrounded Fu Yen-Ch'ing, a Tang Dynasty general, in barren desert country, causing the small Chinese force much hardship for want of water.

As the wells which the Chinese soldiers bored were found to have run dry, the men had no choice but to squeeze lumps of mud from which to suck out the moisture. Many thus died of thirst.

At last Fu Yen-Ch'ing exclaimed: "We are indeed desperate. Yet it would be far better to die fighting for our country than to be taken into captivity by our enemy!" His aide, Tu Chung-Wei, seeing a strong gale blowing then from the northeast and darkening the air with dense dust clouds, suggested waiting until the passing of the storm before ordering a final attack.

Another officer, Li Shou-Cheng however disagreed: "They are many while we are few, but if we are to attack now in the midst of this sandstorm, they will not be able to make out our disadvantage. Thus, if we fight fiercely, victory will be ours since we have the wind as our ally."

Fu Yen-Ch'ing decided to act on the latter's advice and ordered his troops on a sudden and savage attack which was totally unexpected by the Khitans, and thus succeeded in routing the barbarians and breaking through to safety.

OF IGNORANT COMMANDERS WHO KNEW NOT THE *ART OF WAR*

A. Duke Hsiang

During the Spring and Autumn Period (722BC to 481BC), Duke Hsiang of Sung was occupying a strong position on one side of a river while the Zhu troops were still attempting to cross it.

The Sung Minister of War then approached Duke Hsiang, saying: "The enemy is many while we are few. I would thus request your permission to attack before they completely crossed the river," but the Duke refused to grant his permission.

After the Zhu soldiers had all crossed the river but were still disorganised, the War Minister again requested permission to attack "before the enemy can draw up formations." Again, Duke Hsiang refused.

When at last the Duke gave the order to attack, his own ignorance of warfare and his stubbornness in refusing to heed his War Minister's advice resulted in the defeat of the Sung army and he himself being wounded in the thigh.

B. Yuan Shao

Coming to the end of the Han Dynasty (207BC to AD220), when several warlords contended for power, Liu Pei (who later became King of Shu) was defeated by Ts'ao Ts'ao and fled to Yuan Shao for refuge.

Yuan, a highly egoistic man, wished to fight against Ts'ao Ts'ao but his aide, T'ien Fang advised:

"To go against a skilled strategist like Ts'ao Ts'ao is dangerous. It is better to delay and keep him at bay for the moment while you consolidate your positions along the mountains and rivers within your four prefectures. On the outside, seek alliances with other powerful lords while within, pursue an agro-military policy. Only then shall crack troops be used to strike at Ts'ao Ts'ao where he is unprepared. Attack his right, and when he moves to defend the right, attack his left, and so on thus exhausting him by keeping him to be constantly on the move."

Yuan, who was arrogant of his strength and also being impatient by nature, disregarded T'ien Fang's advice and was thus defeated in the subsequent battle.

SUN TZU AND MANAGEMENT

Khoo Kheng-Hor

From the author of *War At Work: Applying Sun Tzu's Art Of War In Today's Management* now comes another polished gem.

Sun Tzu And Management is the author's response to the overwhelming positive feedback he has received from readers for his first book. It is meant to be a detailed textbook for practising managers and is filled with practical ideas and examples drawn from his exposure in senior management positions during the past twelve years.

Khoo Kheng-Hor's book will explain among other things, the applicability and strategic significance of the *Art Of War*; self-development as an employee and as a boss; management of the internal environment, including office politics; and the relevance of Sun Tzu's principles in our dynamic and highly competitive world today.

Functional audit, SWOT analysis, environmental scan, product life cycle, strategy formulation and implementation—they are all here in this must-read book!

ISBN 967 968 404 5
Softcover

Sun Tzu's
ART OF WAR

Translated by Hwang Chung-Mei
Edited by Khoo Kheng-Hor

Recognised as the oldest, the best and the most popular military treatise of all time—the *Art Of War* has been studied by world leaders, military strategists, businesspersons and executives worldwide through the ages to this day.

Why are the Japanese companies today so renowned for their excellence and unsurpassed success in business? Because their executives study and practise Sun Tzu's principles! It is time we catch up with them; it is time we go back to the basics; it is time we pay serious attention to the *Art Of War* and understand: "Know yourself, know your enemy; your victory will be certain. Know Heaven, know Earth; your victory will be complete."

The principles in the *Art Of War* will provoke much thought and will be an invaluable aid to those who desire to succeed in their life, career and business.

This edition by Pelanduk Publications has been specially published so that readers everywhere may benefit from this ancient wisdom.

ISBN 967 978 403 7
Softcover